CHARITY SHOPPING

AND THE THRIFT LIFESTYLE

by Lettice Wilkinson

MARION BOYARS PUBLISHERS

LONDON • NEW YORK

Published in 2009 in Great Britain and the United States by
MARION BOYARS PUBLISHERS LTD
24 Lacy Road, London, SW15 1NL

www.marionboyars.co.uk

Distributed in Australia and New Zealand by Tower Books, Pty Ltd,
Unit 2, 17 Rodborough Road, Frenchs Forest, NSW 2086, Australia

Printed in 2009
10 9 8 7 6 5 4 3 2 1

The publishers have made every effort to secure permission for the reproduction of extracts and to check that the information included in this book is accurate at the time of going to print.

A CIP catalogue record for this book is available from the British Library.
A CIP catalog record for this book is available from the Library of Congress.

10 digit ISBN: 0 7145 3149 9
13 digit ISBN: 978 0 7145 3149 6

Set in Goudy Old Style 10pt
Printed by SNP Leefung, China

Cover design by Alice Marwick
Cover photograph and photographs of UK charity shops throughout by Lettice Wilkinson.
US and Australia - various, with permission.

CHARITY SHOPPING

AND THE THRIFT LIFESTYLE

by Lettice Wilkinson

MARION BOYARS PUBLISHERS

LONDON • NEW YORK

CONTENTS

OTHER

Accessories

Gift

Electrical & White Goods

Childrenswear

Art & Craft

Introduction: A Virtuous Economy

I wrote *Charity Shopping* with a focus on the UK – the country in which I live and where the charity shop is most familiar to me – but the book includes sections on New York City and Sydney, which look at how the charity shop model has adjusted to different contexts. In the United States, (non-profit) thrift store shopping has become so popular that it has earned the slang term 'thrifting'. Australia, where the charity shop is known as the 'op (opportunity) shop', has also seen significant growth in the sector. Although it has always been associated with basic need, the charity shop has come to play an increasingly dynamic role in our society and attracts an ever-growing diversity of customers stretching right across the social spectrum. It is the most innovative of these outlets that this book aims to highlight, hopefully for the benefit of the charities as well as the avid charity shopper. *Charity Shopping* guides the reader through a series of shops, by category, and includes images and personal accounts of the charity shop experience today, from the largest national charities to local hospices.

The charity shop is a recognisable feature of every UK high street. It is a social enterprise that has developed in the religious tradition from its conception in the spirit of wartime thrift and community support through to its present position as a flourishing culture which has adapted brilliantly to the changing demands made on it by competitive thrift opportunity in commercial retail. Britain is the developed world's biggest market for second-hand clothes and, burgeoning during the 1980s and 90s, charity shop sales are currently worth around £550m a year. After business and operating costs, all remaining income from charity shop sales is used in accord with the organisation's stated charitable purpose. Of the combined profit generated by registered charity shops, it is estimated that £110 million reaches the vital causes.

The first Oxfam shop in the UK opened on Broad Street, Oxford in 1948. Originator of the modern charity shop, Oxfam has built up a formidable retail empire, with over 800 shops in operation by the end of the 1980s – at the time representing half of the market. It has become Britain's best-known charity, although its retail network has not significantly expanded in twenty years, whilst the sector has grown to include some 7,000 charity shops. Few shops find themselves competing directly for donations or customers and, in fact, strategically group together in location to attract 'destination' shoppers. The growth of charity retailing has raised public awareness of the numerous causes, in the UK and worldwide, that need financial support.

Oxfam has continually pioneered new retail strategies, to adapt and survive in the ever-changing marketplace. It is therefore quickly blamed as well as praised, inextricably linked with the historical successes and failures of charity retail. Indeed, other charities use Oxfam as a yardstick against which to compare themselves and to both condemn and emulate key developments in the business. During my research I came to the conclusion that the public perception of the charity shop is often outdated, relating to strategic shifts in business in the 1990s, such as centralisation, that have since been reversed or revised.

Some charity shops sell a limited range of new, 'bought-in' goods, which may be branded by the charity or have a connection with the cause that the charity supports. Oxfam stores, for example, sell fair trade food and crafts. Other shops sell supplies and decorations themed to seasonal celebrations or stock goods that are particularly appropriate to their immediate location. Local businesses affiliate themselves with the charity shop by donating obsolete stock, which avoids disposal and tax costs on such items. Charity shops are required to sell wholly or mainly donated goods in order to retain their status as serving a 'charitable purpose'. Commonly it sells mainly (around 93%) second-hand merchandise, donated by and sold on to the public to raise funds for the parent charity.

Once deemed undignified, unsanitary or even haunted by their past lives, second-hand goods are now widely accepted and their currency has soared in value on the international market by more than seventy per cent in the past few years. The vintage clothing market in particular has prospered alongside changing social attitudes, to become a multi-million pound industry. The charity shop has become increasingly aware of its assets, providing discarded fashions for customers looking to emulate the vintage 'look' of high-profile trend-setters. It presents the opportunity for affordable experimentation with mix-and-match identities, allowing customers to make a more inventive statement through out-of-sync styling. Its unpredictable array of goods blows apart the standard taxonomies of mainstream retail and offers surprise juxtapositions that fire the imagination to the creative possibilities for the appropriated use of objects, up-rooted from their original context.

The off-sales department store now offers the type of 'dig-and-delve' shopping experience once unique to the charity shop, constituting just one of the many challenges with which the charity shop has been forced to deal over the past decade. The prevalence of low quality, disposable fashions from budget chain stores has greatly affected donations, and this type of clothing is very hard to sell on in second-hand condition, leaving the shops in desperate need of higher quality donations. Charities have also attributed a steady decline in valuable donations to the rise of online auction sites that make it easy for the private individual and potential charity shop donor not only to research the international market value of their items but also to realise, for personal profit, the market price in a worldwide network. Discount retailers have colonised the British market in recent years and have significantly impacted on charity shop sales. In response, the charity shop has shifted in emphasis towards more lucrative niches, employing profit-share, two-tier and specialism strategies and pooling resources, in order to maximise profits and redeem its share of the market.

Charity shops benefit from tax concessions, funded by central government. Further tax rate relief is available at the discretion of local authorities. For many years charity shops have been recycling in large volumes and there is now an increasing recognition of the official contribution that the charity shop makes as a recycling and reuse facility towards reducing the volume of items that go to landfill. Mutually beneficial partnerships are now being established with local authorities in the form of recycling credits. Growing public concern for the environment and the provenance of manufactured goods have made the charity shop more relevant than ever in the current retail landscape.

Supplementing their inherent virtues, charities have always been inspired by the need to find new ways of incentivizing support for their shops. They increasingly employ professional retailers to manage their chains, with backgrounds in successful retail corporations such as Topshop, Mothercare, Next and Marks and Spencer. Charity shops operate through limited trading companies to enable the charity to employ an executive strata of staff, which helps to generate a higher income overall.

Although there has been an increase in the number of paid staff in recent years, the majority of people working in the charity shop are volunteers. There are more than 120,000 volunteers nationwide, and some shops are run entirely by volunteer staff. Where the profiles in this book quote a member of staff, they are only referred to by name if they work in a managing role because they are prepared to take on the responsibility of spokesperson for the charity. Moreover naming individual volunteers might appear to discredit the combined volunteer effort. Whilst often going far beyond the call of duty, the shop manager now, more often than not, occupies a paid role. It is the unnamed volunteers who are the heroes in this story, dedicating as much as all of their time to working for the charities for rewards other than remunerative and often personal. I would like to take this opportunity to recognise their essential work in making the charity shop not only a viable but also a successful enterprise.

The charity shop is a unique institution that operates within the crossover of public service and private enterprise and at times seems to harbour conflicting interests. It is generally regarded as fulfilling two roles, fundraising for the chief charity and at the same time supporting its local community by providing affordable goods. The fact that it relies heavily on public patronage means that it must address demands for greater financial accountability and transparency in business, and a perceived 'glass ceiling' on charity shop pricing reflects the community's sense of entitlement to benefit from the exchange, with an implicit expectation of public service in return for its support. Shops rumoured to hold back desirable stock to sell directly to dealers or collectors have created a polemic on the issue of privileged access in what is required to be an egalitarian system.

Where the charity cause is directly concerned with the local community, there is less conflict, but premium prices are widely regarded as undermining the reciprocal altruism on which the institution was founded. It is difficult for the charity shop to guarantee that it fulfills its second fundamental objective without compromising the first. It has a duty to research and recognise the value of its donations to try and achieve the highest prices, out of respect for the gift gesture.

For most people the charity shop is an opportunity to consume cheaply. Staff often receive training on antiques appraisal, designed to identify goods of notable value and price them at a level that is high enough to discourage those who might wish to exploit them for personal profit but lower than those in a commercial antiques outlet. Charging a price that shrinks the average vendor's profit margin is the only way to ensure that such items end up in the hands of people who want them, rather than people who want to profit from them. Moderately priced stock that turns over in a suitable time frame meets both of these goals.

The charity shop might once have been described as a folk institution, based on informal custom and friendly barter. In the days when a typically elderly volunteer staff managed the charity shop, customers enjoyed the benefits of an unprejudiced pricing scheme, implemented by a workforce usually lacking in retail experience, and discrepancies arising from subjective valuations of goods between the generations. Likewise, the charities themselves relied to an extent on the oversights in public donations of notably valuable goods.

The growth of the Internet has provided a common reference facility for the valuation of commodities. Although restrictively time-consuming for the charity shop in administration and labour, the Internet provides a vastly wider consumer base with which to match one-off and valuable items and many charities have opened up their retail division to incorporate online auction sales, siphoning off the best wares to sell on eBay so that the highest prices can be achieved.

The charity shop exists within both the market economy and the gift economy, as a culture that emphasises social rewards in exchange for generosity. It is primarily concerned with redressing inequalities in the conditions of humankind through the circulation and redistribution of goods, within both the local and worldwide community, activating social awareness and moral responsibility whilst successfully generating growing profits within the global business sphere. It provides a framework for this ethic to be put into practice by the integration of self-interest and generosity.

Selling almost wholly second-hand goods and ploughing profits into a worthy cause, the charity shop provides for its customers an alternative or 'ethical' lifestyle. The basic use value of the charity shop has been usurped by leisure shopping and, in its immediate environs, it has escaped an undignified image to become not only a viable option but a desirable place to shop. It is no longer a primary means of support for the poor but also a playground for the privileged and has come to be associated with liberal values and an aversion to excess.

In this book I aim to describe the conventions of the charity shop and identify it as a junction between socio-political, economic and artistic culture, highlighting its creative potential as a catalyst for change. Its dualism has been the key to the charity shop's success, as I have attempted to illustrate, as well as highlighting the importance of preserving this character in order to secure its future.

The charity shop aligns itself with and simultaneously challenges market capitalism, coexisting in a symbiotic relationship with mainstream commerce. It has far-reaching implications in finding a new morality within capitalism, with a good blend of reality and the ideal. It harmonises socialist ideals with the capitalist reality. It allows for selfishness and works with the grain of impulsive human behaviour. It gives people the opportunity to be virtuous, regardless of means. It acknowledges the fact that people need an incentive to be generous and makes it easy for them to be so. I propose that what has been created is a relationship between consumption and the virtuous order – a virtuous economy.

Finally, I would like to draw upon my own experience, to celebrate the charity shop for its innovative and dynamic contribution to society and for its open-ended capacity to accept change. I have used the charity shop for many years, out of both necessity and for leisure. For me it has been a vital resource for fashion, music and literature and has provided me with the opportunity for thrift as well as a creative lifestyle. It has been instrumental in establishing for myself a personal identity against the limited opportunities that the 'mainstream' permits. I propose that, for the active and reflective human being, it is an ideal economic model that renews faith in love and optimism for the future.

CAFÉS
& Tearooms

The Comfortably Numb Lifestyle Café, Joshua Foundation - Cardiff, Wales

Created in 1998 by Sarah Cornelius in memory of her son, the Joshua Foundation offers holidays to terminally ill children with cancer and their families.

Situated on the corner of the traditional Victorian Castle Arcade, directly opposite the castle in Cardiff, is the Comfortably Numb Lifestyle Café, run by the Joshua Foundation. The charity's founder, Sarah Cornelius, explains why she chose to run a café rather than a standard charity shop: 'Because I have always done things differently and I wanted to re-jig the concept of charity shopping.'

Under welcome cover from the Castle Arcade, bright red tables and chairs are set outside the glass-fronted café. The inside is warmly lit, with stained wood flooring, red walls and deep-set sofas. The colour scheme is significant and immediately has a physically stimulating effect. Pop music plays in the background contributing to an atmosphere that is at once lively and relaxing. The main wall of the ground floor café area is covered in large pictures of children, including the inspiration behind the charity and its namesake, Joshua Cornelius, all engaged in various sponsored activities and holiday pursuits. Bringing the cause to mind, the red décor becomes a profound and powerful statement that symbolises love as well as sacrifice. 'The colours simply reflect my desire for a happy, relaxed environment which is about living!' Sarah explains. She reveals to me her choice to channel all her emotional energy into this enterprise. 'The name originally is a Pink Floyd song and it sums up how I feel after losing my son.'

The café operates a bar-counter service, with refreshments displayed directly opposite the entrance, designed to tempt the stream of shoppers passing by the front door. Customers take their tray to their preferred seating area, each region providing a different ambience. The café is spread over three floors. In the basement there are sofas, books and a basket full of board games and toys, provided for families to congregate with plenty to occupy the children. Upstairs, throw-cushions furnish a bay window bench that overlooks the arcade for more contemplative relaxation.

The food is freshly prepared by a group of paid kitchen staff and the menu is extensive. I buy a Red Leicester and Crispy Bacon sandwich for £4.10 and a soft drink for £1.20. The prices are not cheap but there are sufficient reminders throughout the space of how profits are spent. Sarah is aware of the expectations of the customer, 'We compete by keeping our prices in line with those of the big guys, which people are happy to pay. We offer generous food and a good atmosphere in return.' Whilst many of the customers are regulars to the café, with shoppers and workers familiar with its fundraising intentions, there is also a high proportion of visiting tourists who come straight from the coach stop directly outside.

At night Comfortably Numb operates as a bar, with a licence to sell alcohol, and hosts various music events on a regular basis, to attract new business. It recently presented the 'Miss Wales' and 'Mr Wales' events and has linked up with the Welsh College of Music and Drama to hold monthly music nights for students, designed to offer a venue in which to play music but also to raise further awareness of the Joshua Foundation's cause. High-profile patrons include the ex-international Welsh rubgy player JJ Williams, whose firm completed the building works on the unit. There are plans to open more cafés including one in Swansea, along with diversification of the charity business to incorporate a hairdresser. In light of the current economic situation, however, the charity is not pushing the expansion for the time being.

ADDRESS 47/49 Castle Arcade, Cardiff, Wales CF10 1BW TELEPHONE 029 2023 3723 OPEN Monday to Saturday 9am - 5pm - open late variously

Hospices Of Hope Tearooms - Otford, Kent

Dedicated to relieving the suffering of terminally ill adults and children in Romania and surrounding countries.

Through the narrow entrance to the teashop there is at first a small retail area selling discernibly new goods in the way of gifts and craft ornaments, with an emphasis on garden ornamentation. There are reproductions of old-fashioned tin goods for the garden and a selection of tasteful floral-print wash-bags and aprons, to satisfy the consumer yearning identified by high street retailers such as Laura Ashley and Cath Kidson. Genuine vintage pieces can be found in the Hospice's antiques shop across the high street (see 'Antiques & Collectables').

Opposite the shop area and café counter, in the middle section of the floor, there are more new goods, toys and gifts, including rotating racks of greeting cards. Gift-styled goods offer an attractive profit margin to any charity shop looking to subsidise operations as a Limited Company. By introducing a restricted selection of these goods for sale in the tea shop the charity gives customers a suitable opportunity to shop whilst taking time over their refreshments. This eases pressure on the shop to find appropriate and attractive second-hand goods to sell from day-to-day, instead channelling all the charity's quality donated goods across to its specialist shop. It also avoids the unsanitary associations of second-hand goods in a dining environment.

At the back the shop transforms into a simple café interior with heavily varnished pine furniture, incorporating the service counter. The ceiling is clad in further pine tongue-and-groove boards, which combines with the exposed structural beams and columns of the original interior to give the area rustic warmth. Together with the second, subsidiary room, seating for sixteen people is provided, and there is also a garden, the views on to which are diffused by net curtains and framed by basic floral drapes. Customer toilets are external, converted from a coal shed and original outside toilet. There is provision for children and babies in the café seating area and changing facilities are available.

The lunchtime 'specials' menu is written up in white chalk on a blackboard, next to the counter. The café is open for morning coffee at 10am, and soups, quiches, salads and sandwiches are served between 11:30am and 2:30pm. Classic cream teas are, of course, also on the menu, priced at £3.85, advertised on an individual laminated menu that sits on each of the tables. The staff, busy preparing food on a quiet afternoon, are on view through a habitually open door to the side kitchen.

The main draw of the tearooms is the homemade cakes on offer. *Time Out* magazine mentions them in one of its 'Country Walks' sections and they are popular with local residents. Shortbread biscuits are presented in boiled sweet jars and under net-covered baskets at the counter. Homemade sponge cakes, loaves and flapjacks are kept chilled in a display-case fridge built in to the side of the counter, and a further tall, freestanding fridge opposite keeps the café well stocked with confectionary. Whole cakes and quiches are wrapped in cling film and stored in view with great care and efficiency.

Three traditional shelving units stand side-by-side to take up one wall of the main tearoom, and are stacked high with homemade jams, authenticated by their hand-written labels and cotton jam pot covers. The assumption is that this café is an innovative enterprise that puts to good use the hobbies and skills of an elderly or homely volunteer force. The jam on sale is not, as one might imagine, made by volunteers but is in fact bought in from a local cottage industry.

Decisions have been made in the basic styling of this interior to appeal to the traditional expectations and romantic impulses of a country tearoom clientele, though this aesthetic is somewhat limited by the budget of a relatively small-scale charity organisation, run by a volunteer force. The entrepreneurship of the Hospices of Hope Tearooms, stretches further than its immediate resources, to combine forces with cottage industry and engage local production on a domestic scale. This concurs with a growing public interest in 'slow food' and locally or responsibly sourced produce. To be able to enjoy home-baked goods is an unusual privilege in a time of industrialised global food production.

ADDRESS 11a High Street (opposite Hospices of Hope antiques shop), Otford, Kent TN14 5PQ TELEPHONE 01959 524 322 OPEN Monday to Saturday 10am - 4:00pm

The Coffee Bar, Heart of Kent Hospice - Maidstone, Kent

Supporting up to 280 patients, plus their families and carers, the services offered by Heart of Kent Hospice are free of charge. It currently costs £2.5m per year to provide this care and Heart of Kent has to raise £1.8m from the community that it serves..

The entrance to the Heart of Kent Hospice shop is set back from the street in the dim forecourt of Starnes Court, in a commercial area of Maidstone town centre signposted by the town council as 'shops of unusual interest'. Unique amongst its ten shops, The Coffee Bar was set up in 1992 by Trading Company manager Sheila Burton, who came to the charity with extensive experience in charity shop management as well as high street retail.

The shop area is spacious and comprises two large rooms on the ground floor of the building and a further retail space upstairs, above the central open-plan café area. The entrance room is lively, selling lots of toys, games, sports equipment, gifts and greeting cards. Random shelving units stand against one another around the room, accommodating videos and a decent collection of books, including many for children. Jewellery and polished silverware is set amidst a display of shells and draped fabrics in a small cabinet and in open boxes on the front desk. The counter is also piled high with bestsellers and has a vintage display of books including the first 1960s edition of the *Blue Peter* children's television programme annual.

A wide passageway and thoroughfare to the café area has room for a further row of shelving units, displaying bric-a-brac such as dolls in their presentation boxes, jewellery boxes and individual ring and necklace boxes, pictures, cooking dishes, vases and ornaments. At the end of the corridor two adjoining rooms extend around the corner of the building. An open kitchen is painted a lemon yellow and the counter is clad with tongue-and-groove pine panelling, offering scones and spiced current buns under clear plastic domes. Four microwaves sit along the back shelves, indicating the limited refreshments available. The 'coffee bar' classification, I discover, is something of a misnomer in that there is no coffee machine. Three volunteers in aprons make hot drinks, sandwiches, salads and anything on toast. The café is renowned for its cheese on toast. Customers readily offer to make cakes for the café but no pre-prepared food can be brought on to the premises for sale, according to the cross-contamination risks dictated by Health and Hygiene standards.

A group of nine customer tables are covered in patterned plastic tablecloths, each adorned with a vase of Chrysanthemums. Leafy houseplants filter the light that comes in through the back window, across the framed prints covering the back wall. An Edwardian patterned paper frieze runs around the top of the walls and the floor is carpeted, here and throughout the rest of the shop, unifying the decor. Surrounded by displays of kitchenware and crockery, including a dresser supporting a full dinner service, the setting is intimate and homely. When I visit the café it is busy with many of its regular customers, one volunteer points out. She keenly expresses a fondness for her 'regulars'. 'We don't profess to be councillors but sometimes people just need a chat. We look out for our regulars. You become quite close,' she adds. She continues to tell me about volunteering after retirement. 'Working here is a stepping stone to getting back into a job, getting confidence back, mixing with people and keeping up with life,' she says.

Continuing on up the stairs, there is a final department of clothing and bed linen. Every available part of the shop is used to sell the merchandise, including the stairwell shelf, where teddies and freestanding picture frames sit, echoing the stereotype windowsill display of an elderly household. There is an extensive men's section above. Shirts have remained in their original packets. There are ties, caps and a fur felt trilby hat, along with a large amount of women's accessories. All the clothes are in keeping with the current season. Plastic garden chairs are made into comfortable customer seating with cushions. Children's clothes are absent because, I am told, they do not sell. The assistant believes this is because second-hand clothes have not completely shaken their unsanitary stigma and parents prefer to buy new clothes for their children.

ADDRESS Heart of Kent Hospice, 3/4 Starnes Court, Union Street, Maidstone, ME14 1EB TELEPHONE 01622 693 858 OPEN Monday to Saturday 9:30am - 4pm

Visitors enjoy tea and cake at Chest, Heart and Stroke Scotland (CHSS) Coffee Shop, Inverness ADDRESS 9 Mealmarket Close, Inverness IV1 1HS (opposite the regular CHSS charity shop) TELEPHONE 01463 713 433 OPEN Monday to Saturday 9.30am - 3.30pm

A corner in the basement at The Comfortably Numb Lifestyle Cafe in Cardiff (see page 14).

Hospices of Hope, Tonbridge is located on the first floor of the Tonbridge charity shop, which is close to Tonbridge Castle. The shop also has a extensive book section with tables and chairs provided for browsing in comfort. ADDRESS 136 High Street, Tonbridge Kent TN9 1BB TELEPHONE 01732 771 919 OPEN Monday to Saturday 9:30am - 4:30pm

NEW YORK

Housing Works Bookstore Café - Soho, Manhattan

Fighting the twin crisis of AIDS and homelessness, Housing Works donates its proceeds to AIDS charities whilst at the same time encouraging a return to work for people who are HIV positive and at a disadvantage in terms of their employment status.

Located on Crosby Street, one block east of Broadway between Houston and Prince in the Soho district, the Housing Works Bookstore Café is positioned to attract customers looking for solace from a busy shopping and working area. Celebrating its 10th anniversary, this branch of Housing Works is one of nine outlets throughout the five boroughs that brand themselves 'a unique destination in both retail and social entrepreneurship'. David Thorpe, Director of Communications, emphasises the importance of their relative financial independence: 'The Thrift Stores were created to create jobs for our clients and generate revenue that didn't make us beholden to politicians or funders.' He believes that the stores have something particularly special to offer their locality, and continues: 'The very successful Housing Works Bookstore Café, along with the Thrift Shops, fills a unique niche in New York City's retail landscape.' The charity has recently expanded its operation, opening two satellite cafés at New York University.

Following its opening in 1998, the bookstore quickly attracted loyal fans who helped to form a board of literary insiders to promote the shop. Managed, in part, by a committee of writers, ten years later the shop has evidently established itself as a hotspot for New York's literary community. It hosts frequent readings, panel discussions, and parties for the major publishers as well as magazines, from *Lucky* to *The New Yorker*. It has also been featured in several films and television programmes. The shop often closes early for special events, including privately organised functions and projects, as the space is available for hire. The Works is a non-profit catering and events firm that offers packages to clients who seek to link business and philanthropy.

For the past five years, the bookshop has launched itself as a venue for live music, under the direction of music writer Alan Light. High-profile musicians have performed here between concerts at the city's prestigious music halls. 'Live From Home' is a monthly benefit concert series, recently celebrating its fifth anniversary with a performance by rock 'n' roll legend John Mellencamp, which continues to bring in a relevant and enticing mix of up-and-coming and celebrated musicians. The shop has hosted more than one hundred and thirty acclaimed acts to date. Seating is unreserved and limited, and tickets can be purchased in advance, online. Events attract contributions from sponsors, including on-going support from First Act Guitars. Whole Foods

Market Bowery is the Official Beer Sponsor of Live From Home.

The store puts on an Open Air Book Sale every autumn, which takes over Crosby Street. Its success has led the organisation to continue to conduct the fair biannually, starting this year with a second spring sale. A party invariably accompanies a sale, which is further PR for fundraising. Fifty signed books by authors including George Saunders, Mary Gaitskill, Jonathan Safran Foer and Paul Auster were last put up for silent auction. Emerging and well-known artists and writers are invited to perform as part of the shop's vital reading series, with previous participants including Sam Lipsyte, Mary Gordon and Lynne Tillman.

The Soho Bookstore Café occupies a large space in a historic downtown building, with twenty-foot high ceilings and mahogany panelled walls and bookshelves. It boasts a stock count of over 45,000 new and used books. The shop does not catalogue the majority of its books, which can hinder the search for a specific title in such a setting, although the volunteer staff are impressively knowledgeable about the stock and also make it accessible to the computer literate shopper by offering advice and sales via email. An Internet sales division is growing, and the shop now sends books and music all over the world. There is an extensive collection of rare, unusual, collectable, out-of-print, and first edition books for sale, and an inventory for these valuable books is available online at abe.com. At the shop, books are competitively priced, and the stock is often rotated.

The $1 and $0.50 bins are popular and considered by some customers to be better than those at The Strand bookshop, with a good selection that is compressed into a reasonable size. Bargain books are also stacked on small carts, parked throughout, and these are roughly organised by genre, with the exception of some fiction hidden in amongst scholarly dissertations. Recent literary magazines are available, for $2 a piece. Used books in 'like new' condition line the walls. The shop makes good use of the space, with a decent selection of titles. Every book, record, CD and DVD on the shelves has been donated. Whilst publishers and reviewers often donate new books, the shop depends heavily on individual customer donations, with the majority of second-hand books on sale given by the public.

Two spiral staircases lead to an upstairs mezzanine area. There is plenty of seating at the tables and free WiFi access is available. The relaxed and peaceful atmosphere attracts students and individuals to study and work here, with laptop computers. When reviewed in the *Village Voice*, regulars reported that the crowds then came in droves to the Bookstore Café. Some customers complained about those who monopolise the seats and tables and the issue has been addressed by the management, with small cards placed on stands that ask for people not to do so. The café further encourages visitors to spend time in the shop. It is staffed by volunteers and offers sandwiches, soups and salad as well as coffee and pastries, throughout the day. An alcohol license allows the sale of beer and wine.

ADDRESS 126 Crosby Street, New York, NY 10012 TELEPHONE +1 212 334 3324 OPEN Monday to Friday 10am - 9pm, Saturday and Sunday 12pm - 7pm

Memorial Sloan-Kettering Cancer Center - Upper East Side, Manhattan

Founded in 1946 to raise funds for Memorial Sloan-Kettering Cancer Center, the Society is a volunteer organisation dedicated to promoting the wellbeing of patients, supporting cancer research and providing public education on the prevention, early detection and treatment of cancer.

For more than fifty-five years, the Memorial Sloan-Kettering Thrift Shop has been a vital part of the charity's fundraising programme, helping to raise over $75,000,000 for the Cancer Center. Although it has been at its current location for over twenty years, keeping in line with its contemporary Upper East Side boutiques the shop has maintained an immaculate exterior, which is currently painted a smoky black colour and adorned with a giant canopy over the front window. The standard of decoration extends seamlessly to the interior, ensuring that an upmarket crowd feels comfortable shopping here and demonstrating that the shop is a befitting repository for their valuable donations. Aluminium and glass cabinets are suspended against stark white walls with contrasted black rack shelving, and a simple brown carpet runs throughout. Featured regularly in magazines and newspapers, the store is known for being a beneficiary of public donations of the highest quality designer and vintage clothing, home furnishings,

accessories, children's clothing, books, and artwork. In a recent *New York Times* 'Style' section article this shop was greatly praised for its fair prices in respect of the superiority of its stock, as well as for the friendliness of its staff.

Three rooms lead on from one another in this large ground floor retail unit, each one displaying furniture and spot lit from above. Racks of clothes sit neatly in line against the walls, homeware is laid out on the shelves or on tables for browsing and there are many paintings, set high up on the walls, which are noticeable immediately on entering and throughout the store. Lurid floral rugs are laid out on the ground and, treated individually, lend themselves to some remarkable displays that show off merchandise to the utmost effect. Of particular note is the jewellery counter, which is an impressive four cases long and set against a wall of scarlet, emerald and glossy black leather handbags, grouped together by colour. It is crammed with every kind of necklace, brooch and bracelet imaginable and many items are still in their boxes, appearing like the casual castoffs of wealthy local residents replete with adornments. Costume jewellery sits happily amongst the more expensive pieces, and a huddle of decorative perfume bottles at the front of the counter are presented for glamorous styling for the dressing table.

Customers heading on through to the very small 'designer room' at the back will find the shop's main attraction. Entire rails are dedicated to recognisable designers. A two-piece Givenchy dress and several Chanel suits are apparent immediately. Big-name brands that are gently worn are priced comparably to immaculate, museum quality pieces by perhaps currently less fashionable or obscure couture houses. Prices are slightly higher than the average thrift outlet but still lower than most vintage stores. Donna Albericao, reporting for the *NYT* in 2007, picked out for herself 'a pair of immaculately tailored late 60s Gucci clam diggers ($150) in khaki canvas with a matching head scarf...'

Albereco goes on to comment, 'Because the clothing in it has been "presorted," the designer room offers a perfect initiation for the novice thrifter lacking the confidence, and perhaps the stomach, to comb through the crammed standard-issue. Yet the editing process remains idiosyncratic enough to ensure that old hands will not feel deprived of sport.' The proportions of the room and the fact that there is just one changing room make shopping here an unusually convivial experience. As women wait to try on items, their attention naturally turns to fellow customers and their finds. The shop seems to have made fables for itself and there are rumours of customers being greeted by rapturous applause when emerging from the fitting room in a fairytale haze of new found glamour. One silver-haired saleslady is known to have read aloud to the grand dames of Manhattan, queuing with armfuls of Chanel for the changing room, from a donated copy of *Elizabeth Taylor: My Love Affair With Jewelry*.

Debbie Grogan, one-time director for the shop, says that her customers traditionally favour Chanel and Halston, which are two labels that appear to be selling at a premium over others and marry the store's location with the consensus of taste in its immediate catchment. 'We cater to a more upscale crowd,' she is reported to have said, 'A Chanel jacket is still going to cost $350, which may seem expensive...but it was originally $3,000, and the expert shopper will see that it's a bargain immediately.' The shop is a well-known treasury of choice womenswear. Famous designers themselves have been known to visit, to look specifically for their own old pieces. Long-term patron and frequent visitor Geoffrey Beene left his valuable archive to Memorial Sloan-Kettering, so his clothes would be hung back on the same racks which he once picked them from. Celebrity customers are also regulars and further endorse the operation.

Because the Cancer Center has included amongst its supporters over the years some of the city's wealthiest and most socially prominent women, the pieces collectively become intimate artefacts of the privileged lifestyle that is romanticised in fiction and represented in the press. Before her death in 2005, Nan Kempner, whose extensive wardrobe was the recent subject of an exhibition at the Metropolitan Museum, bequeathed Memorial Sloane-Kettering the entire contents of her closets, featuring classic designers such as Mainbocher, and particular favourites Yves Saint Laurent and Bill Blass. These are just a few of the labels that can be found at the store's much anticipated 'openings' each year, in the spring, autumn and year-end holiday season. Customers have been known to queue for hours outside to ensure that they make it through the door ahead of the crowds.

ADDRESS 1440 Third Avenue (between 81st and 82nd Streets), New York, NY 10028 TELEPHONE +1 212 535 1250 OPEN Monday to Friday 10am - 5:30pm, Saturday 11am - 5pm

Cure Thrift Shop · East Village, Manhattan

With support from The Diabetes Research Institute Foundation Cure Thrift Shop opened in 2008. It raises money for The Diabetes Research Institute (DRI), a center of excellence at the University of Miami Miller School of Medicine and recognized world leader in cure-focused diabetes research.

The Cure Thrift Shop opened its doors to a 6,000 square-foot Manhattan emporium at the end of July 2008. In preparation, the shop began to accept donations in May, adding to a basic collection of choice pieces that Liz Wolff, founder and shop manager of Cure Thrift, had accumulated over the year. A self-professed 'fourth generation garbage picker and thrift shop junkie', Liz describes her weekends as a child spent at garage sales in the early mornings with her mother and sisters, learning about antiques and collectables, and her excitement at buying second-hand merchandise, 'giving it a new life'. When she was eleven years old, she was diagnosed with Juvenile Diabetes. 'I lived a normal, healthy life (knock on wood) and never let diabetes get in the way of my dreams. Three years ago, I decided to work in the thrift shop industry and managed a major Manhattan thrift shop. During my first year there, the store that I managed made $2,000,000. After working at that shop for two years, I decided to open my own thrift shop to benefit my own cause – diabetes research'.

When in 2007 Liz contacted the Diabetes Research Institute Foundation with her idea to open the Cure Thrift Shop, the organisation agreed to support her and since then she has been working hard to realise the project. Taking possession of a large space in the East Village of Manhattan on May 15th she opened the shop six weeks later. It can be found amongst the discreet boutique consignment shops where the perceived elite buy and sell last year's designer clothing, often with the tags still attached. It is Manhattan's newest thrift shop and has enjoyed initial success, perhaps boosted by its novelty value in the area. It sells merchandise under every reusable commodity category, including furniture, designer clothing, antiques, collectables, electricals, books, art and music. Customers can also bid for items online.

To attract valuable goods from the public, the shop advertises the tax deduction potential on all donations. A free furniture collection service is available and can be booked via the website. Inside the shop, the pieces look attractive against the simple, stylish backdrop of the open plan unit, with ample light and plenty of space to navigate around the goods on offer. As well as showcasing the items in the most advantageous light, the profile of the shop helps to give shoppers confidence in the value attributed to its donations.

The ground floor is laid with original, large-scale black and white chequerboard tiles. A mahogany dining table and upholstered armchairs are placed around a fireplace, above which a large mirror and framed pictures hang. Further items of household furniture, in more modern designs, are concentrically placed around the same focus point. There are IKEA bookshelves at the back, against the left-hand wall, along the top of which an eclectic range of dining chairs are lined up. Sitting-room furniture is arranged on an enormous Turkish rug at the back. Along the right side of the shop there are carefully coordinated groups of more unusual and unique pieces, such as children's school desks and chairs in wood and cast-iron designs from the 1950s. There are wooden storage chests on the floor and a large rocking chair. Pairs of table lamps are dotted about the surfaces of the furniture. The music area is lively, with a distinctly kitsch styling, achieved mostly by the retro mannequin busts and the derivative painted artworks on the wall, hanging around the room and above the hi-fi separates that are available to buy.

Upstairs on the mezzanine level there are elegantly presented items of homeware and linen. Electrical items are also for sale. In the basement of the shop there is an impressive clothing department. A pair of mannequins rise up from a circular rail in the stairwell, dressed in 'his and hers' formal 50s apparel. Above each rail are compositions that depict familiar street styles from the late 20th century. A pair of Louboutin shoes is offered at an impressively reduced price of $45. The shop has been widely praised by Internet bloggers as 'a Manhattan thrift shop with Brooklyn prices'.

ADDRESS 111 East 12th Street (between Third and Fourth Avenue), New York, NY 10003 TELEPHONE +1 212 505 7467 OPEN Tuesday to Friday 11am - 7pm, Saturday 10am - 6pm, Sunday 12pm - 5pm

Housing Works - Chelsea, Manhattan

Housing Works is the nation's largest non-profit minority-controlled AIDS service organisation. Its mission is to reach the most vulnerable among those affected by the AIDS epidemic in New York City, primarily homeless persons of colour whose positive HIV diagnoses are complicated by a history of chronic mental illness and/or chemical dependence.

Housing Works was founded by four members of ACT UP's Housing Committee in 1990. They saw a great need to provide medical and other services to homeless people in New York with HIV/AIDS, who at the time were estimated to number 30,000. Operations at Housing Works serve a dual purpose. Not only are all profits geared towards improving the position of AIDS sufferers but the stores also help disadvantaged minority groups who are HIV positive by offering them work. Housing Works' clients who work in the thrift stores are trainees or graduates from the charity's acclaimed 'Second Life' job training scheme. Graduates of the programme are guaranteed a $25,000-a-year job at Housing Works, with full benefits, and the thrift stores employ many of these people.

The shops currently bring in one third of the charity's revenue and last year the stores grossed $11 million – the highest profit total to date. This Chelsea branch is one of seven Housing Works thrift stores and concentrates on furniture sales, although it also has displays of vintage clothing and jewellery. In early August 2006, this flagship shop re-opened after a two month absence. The carpet has been ripped up to reveal the original hardwood floor and the unit opened up to create a total floor space of 4,000 square foot, to house more comfortably the charity's stock of antique furniture and give it a more dramatic backdrop.

Major Housing Works Fashion Events are held at the Chelsea location, and new designer clothing and accessories are donated by major designers to be sold at these evenings. The shop hosts an annual Fall Preview event, featuring the very best clothing that has been cherry-picked and saved for months, stored at the charity's warehouse facility. The shop advertises its goods for sale at 'charitable prices', which are generally seventy per cent off the original retail cost. The sale has proved to be such an attraction that a $10 entry charge has been introduced. This location has also accommodated the Fashion for Action benefit in the past few years.

Merchandise that does not make it into the shops is sold through the warehouse's monthly 'by the pound' sales, where clothing is charged at $3 for a pound in weight, or is sold on to a rag company. The shop aims to present its merchandise with innovative displays and there is a good selection of clothes and furniture. The clothes are upmarket and modern, and most are in good condition. In the furniture department, reported examples of shoppers' finds include a 1940s mirrored vanity unit on sale for $1,200, mid-century Thonet chairs at $150 a piece and a Calvin Klein platinum tableware set at $800. There are also several quality hand-knotted carpets.

The co-ordinators of Housing Works thrift shops believe that the effort invested in a quality presentation of the stores encourages the public to donate a higher calibre of goods than that given to a 'normal' thrift shop. Marea Judilla, head of merchandising, says, 'I think the bottom line is innovation. It's a working process of reacting to materials, evaluating common elements of colour, theme, story, or perhaps the disjunct of elements in the stock. Learning about the history of pieces, components of material and origin enriches the direction of display ideas for windows, mannequins, floor and case set-ups. It is something in constant evolution.' Limitations of budget, time and such variety of donations presents a challenging foundation on which to build. Staff involved with merchandising are encouraged to have their own voice as well as work within the pre-existing standards of the organisation. 'I want art, people, the character of the store, the neighbourhood, the customers, daily life, and "fantasy" to push and pull inspiration for customers and staff,' she continues. She regards the team as 'a mixed bag of artists, very different and very similar,' that create the dynamic for visuals. 'We take our jobs very seriously and collaborate to challenge each other to new heights for visual merchandising.'

The window of the Chelsea shop showcases the items in impressive displays. The shops have been auctioning off items from their window displays long before the boom of the Internet. The Chelsea retail unit has particularly good window-shopping potential, and 'set-ups' were designed to take full advantage of the space, attracting immediate requests from passers-by to purchase items from the increasingly inventive curated displays. In order not to disrupt the sets as the items sold, the paper-based silent auctions were introduced.

For those who do not live nearby, and following the success of eBay, the charity began the online auction division of Housing Works. The online auctions have raised over $5 million since their launch in 2004, making more money for the charity online than the physical outlets, which will always be hindered by expensive rents in the city. The highest ticketed item that has sold on the site is a small landscape painting, which sold for $13,004.51, after bidding started at $45, making more money for the charity than an entire week's worth of sales at the 90th Street store.

ADDRESS 143 West 17th Street (between 6th and 7th Street), New York, NY 10011 TELEPHONE +1 212 366 0820 OPEN Monday to Friday 10am - 7pm, Saturday 10am - 6pm, Sunday 12pm - 5pm

Angel Street Thrift Shop · Chelsea, Manhattan

Since 1997, Angel Street Thrift Shop's proceeds benefit individuals and families affected by Substance Abuse, HIV, AIDS and Mental Illness.

Describing itself as 'A Heavenly Thrift Shop', the charity's website boasts several high-end examples of donated merchandise available from the shop as if they were commonplace: 'From a Toyota Celica, a Wurlitzer piano and exercise equipment to Dansk candle holders, a Rolex watch or baby cribs, you can be sure to uncover hidden, heavenly treasures at Angel Street'. Whilst the stock is clean and has an interesting selection of used clothes and furniture it does not in fact appear to constitute a treasury of such worthy and universally recognised commodities.

On a far more modest level, there is a wide range of products available here to furnish the home and to fill the wardrobe. The store contains a mix of men's and women's clothing, arranged according to colour, furniture, art, decorative accessories and functional utensils. These items are donated by fashion outlets and home furnishing companies as well as individuals, and the mix of new and used, unusual and practical, makes for an enticing shopping experience. There are creaky wooden floors and standard-issue thrift store racks to hang the clothes, which are all displayed with impeccable care and attention. The spare white walls are unadorned except for some cutesy and nostalgic paraphernalia. Elements of the stock are moved around the shop floor from day to day. The layout of the clothing section has recently been re-organised which has thrown up a great many new finds and generated feverish attention from the regular clientele. In this event, the shop has taken the opportunity to increase the prices moderately. Dresses that were once set at around the $30 mark are now $40.

Just across the street from a Housing Works store, Angel Street is yet another thrift shop in Chelsea. With such a large grouping of charity shops on West 17th Street, dubbed as 'thrift shop alley', a visiting shopper might assume that Angel Street could not possibly generate any new interest on the scene. However, when it opened at the end of 1997 its boutique decor soon attracted a clientele looking for high quality merchandise. The operation courted attention from the outset with a grand opening 'China Fun' sale, replete with oriental pieces. The subsequent 'Rooms-Abloom' spring sales event, with the emphasis on gardening, also proved popular. This summer, the charity opened a 10,000 square-foot warehouse in Greenpoint, Brooklyn, with an inventory that included, according to one shopper, three hundred sets of brand new curtains ($165 to $230 each), new photography books and vintage design books.

There is a lot of military clothing in the Chelsea shop, from the standard camouflage kit to sailor tops and officer uniforms. There is also a particularly large selection of fur and leather jackets. There are many pairs of cowboy boots, in addition to all kinds of shoes, hats and bags in the accessories area. Continuing with the Western theme there are also Western-looking shirts and two racks full of T-shirts, set at decent prices. This combination of distinctive and currently popular styles identifies the shop with the trendy vintage boutiques of the nearby Greenwich Village. It is interesting to compare prices to those of the reputedly expensive fashion shops on St. Mark's Place. T-shirts are the same price in Search and Destroy as they are at Angel Street ($5). There is another shop nearby that sells vintage clothing, with a twenty-five per cent reduction sale, and a silk Dior shirt is $40 – again, equitable with the thrift shop prices.

The thrift shops appear to have mediated the prices of the designer clothing market, which are altogether reasonable. At Angel Street, the pieces that are often highly sought after – the elusive international designer labels, such as Vivienne Westwood and Commes Des Garcons – are showcased on mannequins and in the display cases for a certain period of time after their arrival. Clothing of European manufacture apparently sells very well here. A full-length Italian wool coat is $60. A new-with-tags camel hair A-line skirt, also made in Italy, is $20. A Laundry dress is $40. One blogger on the website Yelp discussing the thrift shop makes the point that if a person is prepared to spend $50 on clothes then why not buy something that is one hundred per cent silk or cashmere from a place such as Angel Street for the same price as a new, cheaply manufactured Hennes and Mauritz garment. In the back of the shop, a simple, elegant curtain is provided to hide behind when trying on potential buys.

In the furniture department, there is a magnificent mahogany dresser. Its grand scale must be a handicap for the majority of local thrift shoppers who, I imagine, would be unlikely to fit such a piece in their Manhattan apartment. For this reason perhaps it is here, realistically priced at $250.

ADDRESS 118 West 17th Street, Chelsea, Manhattan, New York NY 10011 TELEPHONE +1 212 229 0546. OPEN Monday to Saturday 10am - 6pm Sunday 12am - 5pm

City Opera Thrift Shop - Gramercy, Manhattan

New York City Opera was founded in 1943 to provide financially accessible opera performances to a wide audience – performances that would reflect the company's commitment to innovative repertory choices and the development of American opera.

This is a highly acclaimed thrift shop, now celebrating its thirtieth anniversary and twenty-five years at its current location. It is currently the only thrift shop in NYC that supports a performing arts institution. Proceeds go to the venerable Lincoln Center company, of which NYC Opera is one of twelve resident organisations.

To maintain its profile, the organisation looks to generate publicity about the shop through special sales and events, seeking listings and articles in NYC newspapers and publications. It also plans an event each year with the assistance of fashion insiders, such as Patricia Field, John Bartlett, Robert Verdi, Rebecca Taylor, Elsa Klensch, Lorry Newhouse, Michael Fink and Phillip Bloch, all of whom have co-chaired the one-night annual shopping occasion called DIVAS Shop for Opera, now in its third year, featuring a collection of donated vintage and designer clothing, accessories, jewellery, home furnishings and other select items at fifty to seventy-five per cent off the recommended retail price. All proceeds from the evening fund the design and creation of costumes for new productions at New York City Opera. All unsold items are made available the next day at the City Opera Thrift Shop.

The charity encourages the donation of quality items by reaching out to those individuals that it considers to be 'art-minded', offering them the opportunity to support the arts through this very practical endeavour. The charity has restrictions on what it is willing to collect from donors, although it is more concerned with what is finally put up for sale. 'Quality is more important than quantity' is the maxim by which it chooses to conduct itself. Donating goods is made as easy as possible for the NYC public and added incentives have been introduced. Direct donations are accepted at the shop, which will also collect free of charge any large items from an address within the five boroughs, usually in three to five working days. Taxi fares are reimbursed up to $10, for smaller donations.

Although City Opera is located near to the thrift shops on West 17th Street and about five other thrift shops within a two block radius, it does not see these shops as competition because it has established a reliable customer base and because it is able to offer a slightly different selection of items, often marked out by their quality or unusual character. These desirable qualities mean goods come at a premium price. One Internet reporter provides some colourful examples, such as Lilian Shore sculptures, for $250. A leather lounge chair with ottoman by Ekornes is $550. The shop too has some unique features. Window displays are created by students from The School of Visual Arts across the street. Many of the staff members are passionate about opera and music and this is reflected in their commitment and motivation. There are a variety of charity shops of this kind in the neighbourhood, and it has become a destination for thrift shopping, which benefits all the shops.

The City Opera Thrift Store receives regular donations of vintage clothing and has become known for its biannual vintage sales, which enjoy high-profile celebrity attendance as well as the vintage fashion seekers. A designer sample sale was held at the beginning of last year. Samples from Jones, Nine West, Latina, Norton, Bandolino, Rena Rowan and W were collected for the event. There is also a Spring Preview event held at the shop. Sales benefit city culture and the leftovers are offered to Goodwill and the Salvation Army, passing on the fruits of its fertile reputation.

Between the publicised events, the shop's regular stock consists of clothing that is suitable for a night out at the NY State Theatre. Blazers, ties and slacks are noticeably worn but nevertheless still wearable for a smart night out. The majority of the merchandise is not more expensive than any other second-hand outlet in the area, dictated by the pricing consensus of all the local thrift shops. There are heavily marked-down fur coats and designer shoes start at $25. Designer duds scattered about the rails make for an entertaining and promising bargain hunt. Upstairs, the goods are less impressive. Half empty shelves carry stray pieces of pressed glassware and there is a small selection of novels, art books and random non-fiction titles, which contrasts with the evident success of its 'vintage' clothing enterprise.

ADDRESS 222 East 23rd Street (near Third Avenue) New York, NY 10010 TELEPHONE +1 212 684 5344 OPEN Monday to Friday 10am - 7pm, Saturday 10am - 6pm, Sunday 12pm - 5pm

Furniture and vintage clothing at Housing Works, Chelsea (see page 33).

Dark blue awning leading into the Arthritis Thrift Shop, Manhattan, Upper East Side ADDRESS 1383 Third Avenue (78th & 79th) New York, NY 10021 TELEPHONE +1 212 772 8816 OPEN Monday to Saturday 10am - 5:45 pm

Scarlet patterned chaise-lounge and other furniture at The Memorial Sloan-Kettering Cancer Centre (see page 28).

A call for donations and window display at the Salvation Army Thrift Store, Williamsburg/Brooklyn. ADDRESS 176 Bedford Avenue, Brooklyn, New York NY 11226 TELEPHONE +1 718 388 9249 OPEN Monday and Thursday 10am - 6:30pm, Tuesday, Wednesday, Friday and Saturday 10am -7pm

SYDNEY

The Peter Pan Op Shop, Barnado's - Paddington

Supporting Barnardo's, the childrens charity, which deals with the effects of neglect and abuse.

The Peter Pan Op Shop Committee is a fundraising organisation that has run a biannual sale of donated goods since 1941. It began in the basement of G.J. Coles on Pitt Street, Sydney, where the sale caused a traffic jam along the street and there were reports of fainting shoppers, desperate to get a bargain. In the following years, the sale moved to other premises, eventually arriving at the town hall in Paddington. After sixty-seven years the Committee has perfected the formula for a successful sale and also claims to have coined the term 'Opportunity Shop', which is now part of Australian jargon.

The Committee is made up of a group of about sixty-five women volunteers, aged between forty and eighty, who work tirelessly throughout the year sourcing and collecting 'pre-loved', new and vintage clothing for the purpose of re-sale, from donors throughout Sydney and the Southern Highlands. The winter sale takes place in May and the summer sale in October, each selling seasonal clothing. The sales run for two to three days and invitations are sent out four weeks prior to the event. An advertising campaign promotes the event in newspapers and on the radio, and the dates are listed on Barnardos' website in Australia. The Op Shop is only one arm of the Committee's fundraising work. It also organises literary lunches, dinners, bridge days and other fundraising activities and the sales are promoted at these events as well.

The team is equipped with a list of regular donors and purchasers, who are contacted by mail prior to a sale to ask them to part with their unwanted clothes. More often than not, people approach the charity unprompted, with donations. The requirements are that all clothes must be in pristine condition, dry-cleaned and of top quality. Designer labels are preferred for best re-sale potential and there is always a decent collection of top name brands, such as Armani, Burberry, Basler, Collette Dinnigan and Lisa Ho, and often include obvious fashion 'mistakes' that come with original labels attached. It has been reported that the Peter Pan Op Shop has such a reliably good selection of vintage clothing that the vintage shops stock up at the sales as well as other Op Shops in Sydney who supplement their collections.

In preparation for a sale, invitations to donors are followed up with a phone call closer to the date to arrange for pick up. Although there is storage space for a limited amount of goods, it is generally reserved for out-of-season clothes that are worth keeping until the appropriate season sale. Before a sale, the majority of the donations are picked up at the beginning of the week and sorted, priced, hung or folded over two long days. Friends of volunteers

– some of whom have experience in retail, vintage or jewellery markets – help throughout the week with setting up and marking prices.

The Peter Pan Op Shop primarily sells women's clothes, although there is always a small selection of men's and children's wear. Also available are shoes, handbags, scarves, gloves, belts and jewellery valued by an expert jeweller. Fur is sometimes offered for sale, depending on the political climate. Prices vary from year to year but the aim is to move the merchandise as quickly as possible and to get the funds efficiently to where they are most needed. Articles range from $2 to $4 for a basic T-shirt to $350 for an Armani evening suit. Goods that are left over are forwarded to other charities such as Anglicare or Wayside Chapel, which have more extensive storage facilities.

Barnardos, Paddington opts to raise funds this way to avoid the costs involved with running a shop, not least of which is the rental of the space and finding enough volunteers to man the operation on a permanent basis. For these two weeks of the year, volunteers are prepared to work extremely hard to raise the funds through the sales. Considering the fact that it holds its sale for as little as six days in total, it is impressive that the charity raises between $90,000 and $100,000 each year. Overheads are kept to a minimum and the City of Sydney Council that owns the town hall has been generous in giving a large discount on the cost of hiring the facility.

The building is a purpose-built Victorian town hall, located on Oxford Street in the heart of the Eastern suburbs of Sydney. Oxford Street is a hub of high street clothes shops mixed with designer boutiques, cafes and restaurants. It has particularly good transport connections, which was a major consideration in choosing the location. For the event, large banners are hung outside on the facade. The sale is held on the first floor in a large cavernous space that was once the ballroom, with ornate ceilings, parquet floor and windows and French-doors all along one side. Opposite there is a smaller room where the jewellery sale is held together with the menswear collection.

Regular shoppers arrive two hours before opening time to queue until the doors open.

Shoes are always popular as well as jackets and trousers. Suits always sell well, as does eveningwear and vintage. Skirts are for some reason unpopular and, although it may vary from one sale to the next, their prices are kept to a minimum to avoid a full rail at the end of the week. Clothes are hung in categorized garment groups. Shoes are displayed on long tables near the entrance, alongside bags. Past the racks of clothes, at the back end, a jumble of clothes marked under $20 is arranged over table-tops, with changing facilities located behind. In the lobby there is a checkout desk and a mailing list for customers who wish to be alerted to future sales and the charity's donation needs.

ADDRESS Paddington Town Hall, Oxford Street, Paddington, Sydney, NSW 2021 TELEPHONE (Barnardo's Australia) +61 (0) 29281 7933

The Bower - Marrickville

The Centre is a co-operative, non-profit, community organisation whose primary business is to divert household and office waste for re-use. It aims to educate the community about the value of waste reduction, provide renovation and re-use craft skills, affordable goods to low income and disadvantaged groups, a source of local employment and advocate sustainable living, involving the community in making these goals part of everyday living.

The Bower is located at the Addison Road Centre for Arts Culture, Community and Environment, in Marrickville. This 258sqm passive solar warehouse is an excellent example of sustainable building practices, and the first of its kind in Sydney, made entirely of straw-bales and recycled materials. Straw-bale building is relatively new in Australia, whilst it has over a hundred years of history in the United States, and only slightly less in New Zealand. This building uses fully recycled materials in its construction: load-bearing posts recovered from demolition sites, roof trusses from the Royal Prince Alfred Hospital refurbishment, five thousand second-hand bricks, second-hand roof sheeting, and all doors and windows salvaged from waste on Sydney streets. Nearly every fixture and fitting in the centre is reused and a rainwater tank is used for washing.

Marrickville is otherwise made up of Victorian and Federation style houses. It is a suburb of the Inner West of Sydney with a significant migrant population dominated by Greek and Vietnamese cultures. There is a visible percentage of young urban professionals living in the area because of the proximity to the Central Business District and also to the University of Sydney, attracting a lot of students in the mix. According to the council's website (2005), 'The area contains one of the highest percentages of artists, cultural workers and arts industries of any local government area in Australia.' The Bower is a charity catering for the immediate demographic. It aims to provide affordable items for low-income earners and disadvantaged groups within the community, and the constituent goods for creative and resourceful living.

Set up by Sydney residents and run as a cooperative of over one hundred and thirty local members, this is an independent community-driven initiative and Limited Company. The co-operative structure was preferred by a number of its original members, who had previous experience of community-based co-operatives in the area. In its early stages, the Bower was a worker style co-operative. As it has evolved, however, it has shifted towards a consumer model. The Bower provides part time employment for around twelve members in its shop and repair centre. It also relies on a flow of volunteers from various programs like Green Reserve, Community Service Orders and Work for the Dole.

The remaining staff are members who pay a small annual fee and commit at least eight hours of unpaid service per year in return for their membership.

It is not always easy for members to find the time to commit to the project and so there are some difficulties maintaining the balance of responsibilities, especially in relation to management. The Centre is working to attract new members so that they can better spread this burden in the future. Fulfilling the labour requirements entitles active members to voting privileges and small discounts on purchases as well as the opportunity to submit goods for consignment sale, access to workshops and Annual General Meetings. Cooperatively, the members (of the public) own and ultimately control the assets of The Bower. They elect the voluntary Board of Directors, who employ an on-site coordinator, who in turn employs the staff for sales, repairs and resource collection.

The Bower repairs and resells a range of goods, from building materials to electrical appliances to household and office furniture. Electrical appliances, including white goods, are tested for safety before resale and minor repairs are made where feasible. The shop uses the local council household clean-ups and rescues and repairs a variety of items that may have otherwise been consigned to the local dump. The warehouse is mainly a repository for furniture and large-scale household goods as well as the miscellany that accumulates at a donation centre. Building materials include doors, bathtubs, basins, scrap-metal, such as piping and fencing, and scrap timber. Architectural salvage comprises fireplaces, timber bookshelves, sash and stained glass windows and there is a great selection of brassware. Homeware is a particularly varied category, including bed bases, tables, suites, chairs, toys, sports equipment, outdoor furniture, musical instruments, mirrors, artwork, jewellery and kitchenware.

The Bower promotes itself with the line, 'Traders of the Lost Artefact', to reflect the sheer range of goods here. Prop Buyers and Art Directors frequently browse and use the op shop, hiring out items at twenty-five per cent of the listed shop price, with a one hundred per cent security deposit. They are often returned in good condition and so The Bower is looking to formalise its prop hire policy to assist the industry in acquiring the use of the rare and unusual items found at the warehouse.

The Bower advocates long-life design, repairable products and the use of sustainable, recyclable materials for appliances and furnishings, through the

support of small-scale operations that produce new products from discarded goods. Consignees use craftsmanship to reinvent goods or recycle scrap materials. Other sympathetic initiatives worldwide are brokered here. A Dutch company sells flat-packed, self-assembly wastepaper bins and magazine racks made from large billboard posters. Plates and platters are made from textured glass light diffusers taken from government buildings. Designer Jeff Davis rescues scratched vinyl records and transforms them into functional bowls. A UK company makes timber furniture from cable reels. Textiles and reclaimed inner tubes are remade into accessories. Also available is a range of goods from countries where recycling has been incorporated into the culture out of necessity rather than ideological concern. Traditional tribal crafts use untraditional materials such as PVC coated telephone wire. As one Bower member points out on the website, 'In our grandparent's generation, manufactured items were used over and over again. Labour was cheap, but resources were expensive. Waste dumps from their days were rather light on re-usable items and transformation was a natural expression.'

In its re-use and repair capacity the co-operative works towards a solution for the city's waste 'crisis', diverting household and office items back into the community. It is estimated that a quarter of a million tonnes of household 'hard waste' is generated each year in the south region of Sydney alone, creating a burden on the community in both financial cost and pollution. The Bower calculates that, through both referral and receipt of donated goods, it diverts almost five tonnes of landfill each week from the Sydney metropolitan municipal waste stream, whilst educating the community about waste reduction.

The Bower aims to raise awareness of the value of waste reduction through its education facility and eco-library. Free Internet use is available. This new space at the Centre houses The Bower's extensive collection of books concerning reuse, simple living and DIY. There are many books and journals available on sustainable design, belonging to the Society for Responsible Design (SRD). Lectures, seminars, meetings and workshops are held regularly as part of the overall drive to encourage community awareness of environmentally responsible design and manufacture, promoting the idea that good design is inherently ecologically sound and sustainable. The company is also proactive in the community and works with schools to develop environmental audits. Recycling is only one side of the Cooperative's concern, with repair as its twin. Through the use of its workshop, a 'repair culture' is encouraged within the community. Workshops are provided for Computer Upgrade & Maintenance, Minor Electrical Repair, Simple Construction, and Sanding & Finishing.

Inevitably constrained by space, The Bower offers a Reuse Referral Service to customers in the event that an alternative repository must be found for donated furniture. The RRS becomes a vital dimension of the operation where Occupational Health and Safety regulations place restrictions on goods sold. A database, supported by eleven councils in the Sydney region, lists a wide range of associations, including other charities and community organisations, which are independent of The Bower but equally driven by their commitment to waste reduction. The Bower operates alongside both non-profit and for-profit organisations that repair or recycle goods. One truck runs three days a week, offering free collection, although most customers are happy to make a $5 donation. Delivery charges depend on the area and number of items. The service is currently running a one-year Biodiesel trial in the delivery truck.

ADDRESS The Bower Reuse & Repair Centre Co-op Ltd, Building 34, 142 Addison Road, Marrickville 2204 TELEPHONE +61 (0) 29568 6280 OPEN Monday to Saturday 10am - 5pm, Sunday 10am - 3pm

The Goodwill Charity Card Shop - Central Business District

Operating for over twenty years, The Goodwill Charity Card Shop has been marketing Christmas cards on behalf of various charities and provided them with a specialist retail outlet. The shop serves twelve Australian charities, which each produce and supply their own unique range of Christmas cards. Each group has at least six or more designs of greeting cards and all proceeds go directly to the umbrella organisation. The shop is also linked to combined charities' cards shops in other states.

Premises for the Goodwill Charity Card Shop are found each year, for a period of three months, from the last week of September through to the end of the third week in December, and the charities conduct a sale through this joint venture. Last year the sale was conducted from a Bathhurst Street location in Central Business District. This year it was held in a unit on the eighth floor of the Dymocks Building on the concentrated commercial city street, George Street. The organisation hopes next year to establish a permanent shop location in the CBD area and it is seeking interested parties to provide premises. By letting excess office or storage space to Goodwill, businesses can benefit from exposure to the customers who are attracted through their links with a charitable organisation.

High street shops and Internet retailers fight a fierce battle for business in the greetings card stakes. The high street has been criticised for its 'charity' card dealings, with complaints of retailers promoting sales through charitable affiliations but failing to pass back to the charities a reasonable share of the profits. Each year, charity cards prove popular in sales but it has been reported that as little as two per cent of the card price reaches some charities, with high street stores the worst at passing on the profit. In the worst cases, less than $0.10 in the dollar is passed back to the charity.

The GCCS is staffed entirely by volunteers as are those organisations which participate in the making of the cards, so there are low overhead costs. The Focus Press provides the printing at subsidised prices and – after covering the expenses involved in maintaining a website, as well as the initial, nominal outlay of each charitable group – all the proceeds that are raised from card sales are returned to the charity to fund vital education programmes, research, special projects and other activities. Currently, the Goodwill shop sells greeting cards exclusively, which offer good wishes for Christmas and the New Year. The cards are mostly traditional with verse inscriptions and depict religious as well as secular imagery, including beach scenes, seasonal plants such as Bottlebrush, indigenous and symbolic breeds of birds, and romantic country landscapes in full summer. Prices range from $0.60 to $1 per card. Alternatively there is a Mail Order facility online. All the cards are organised by charitable organisation so that the customer can shop by choosing a cause rather than design.

Christmas is linked inextricably with charity and, during the 'season of goodwill', The Goodwill Charity Card Shop hopes to exploit the massive increase in demand for greeting cards. Last year, it is estimated that Britons sent 1.8 billion greeting cards and around half of these were charity cards. The popularity of charity Christmas cards reflects the win-win situation that motivates customers to buy from non-profit organisations. By buying cards where a proportion of financial outlay goes to charity, a customer supports a 'good cause' and the gift in the form of a greetings card is enhanced by the will to 'do good'.

A volunteer at the GCCS describes the benefits of purchasing from the organisation with the idiom of 'hitting two birds with one stone'. 'By sending Christmas cheer to your friends and loved ones, you are also donating to charities that will benefit humanitarian causes. It is a gift that gives twice,' she says. This emphasises very well the role of the charity shop in a post Judeo-Christian culture. Society is educated historically to charitable giving and the gestures that it necessitates have become, to an extent, a social formality. The practical role of non-profit retail enables the gift exchange to continue. In his article in the *Independent*, promoting charitable giving at Christmas, David Prosser makes the valid point that, 'By putting your money to the best possible use, you can avoid a new-year hangover of guilt about your excessive consumption.'

ADDRESS WEA House, Level 1, 72 Bathurst Street, Sydney NSW 2000 TELEPHONE +61 (0) 41684 7876 OPEN Monday to Friday, 9:30am - 4pm (late September to mid-December)

JOHN GREEN
AHMT
. AJO

ANTIQUES 1988³

STET FORTUNA DOMUS

DONORUM DEI DISPENSATIO FIDELIS

COLLECTABLES

Collectables, Katharine House Hospice - Stafford, Staffordshire

Katharine House Hospice exists for the people of mid-Staffordshire and originated as a result of public demand and support.

At the bottom of the pedestrian Greengate Street, on the corner of Mill Street in Stafford city centre, is Collectables, the Katharine House Hospice shop specialising in the 'unusual and the different'. Nine of their shops are traditional Hospice shops but this and the Yesterdays shop in Stone (see 'Ceramics') both sell 'collectable' goods, such as ceramics and furniture, both antique and contemporary. This means that the stock is made up from the best of the Hospice's donated goods which are sent to these two specialist shops.

The shop has a traditional frontage and the small window means that its display is significantly less dramatic than the pile of eclectic, ever-changing and enticing junk placed outside on the pavement to attract people passing by. This collection appears to suggest that the shop will contain something of interest for everyone. The organic and hotch-potch mix could belong to one person and, out here on the street, looks as if it is about to be taken away by a removal van. Exercise equipment, homeware, records, books, toys and furniture are piled on top of each other as if clambering to attract attention. Regular customers call the shop 'Aladdin's Cave'.

The left side of the shop has two large windows, crammed with polished brass and knick-knacks. It's busy with people and objects, around which the

customer must navigate. Along with furnishings, such as curtains and bed linen, at the back of the shop there is a selection of knitted items in attractive combinations of colours. These hand-crafted pieces look familiar, as if derived from a popular old-fashioned pattern book. I buy a beautifully made 'large' tea cosy, knitted to the traditional scalloped stripe pattern, for £3.50 (small £1.50, medium £2.50).

During my visit the shop assistant brings out several paintings from the back room. In keeping with its reputation for 'collectable' stock, the shop sells lots of old coins, exhibited in a specifically designed display case. There is also plenty of Staffordshire pottery, filling most of the central portion of the shop floor. The more valuable vinyl LPs are kept behind the counter and so I ask to browse through them, only to find one of my price-comparison items – The Beatles' *Red Album*, Trident compilation/1962-66 – is selling here for the highest price I have yet come across, at £30. Records such as this, which regularly appear in the charity shops, are a good marker of a shop's overall pricing policy. Of course, both the edition and the condition of the vinyl play a part in the pricing of an LP, which must be considered in my judgement.

A glass-topped jewellery cabinet on the till-counter houses an attractive collection of costume jewellery. Light shades and lamp shades are hung from the ceiling at the front of the shop, over a cascade of toys, greeting cards and small pieces of furniture such as old card-filing drawers.

ADDRESS 37, Greengate Street, Stafford ST16 2JA TELEPHONE 01785 229 500
OPEN Monday to Saturday 9:15am - 4:45pm, Sunday 10:30am - 4:30pm

The Martlets Hospice - Brighton, East Sussex

The Hospice offers expert and compassionate care, to enhance the quality of life and ease the distress of patients suffering from cancer and other serious conditions and for whom curative treatment is no longer appropriate.

This charity shop occupies a retail unit that was previously a bank and is near the large chain stores, such as TKMaxx, on the busy shopping stretch of George Street. Sheltered under the overhang of the office building above, the shop façade has retained the original features from a time when brushed steel and glass became the popular modern aesthetic. A generously sized stage inside the front window displays some of the shop's more valuable pieces; 1950s chinaware, a chrome tea set, bone-handled cutlery, crystal decanters and old-fashioned telephones set the scene. There are attractive examples of traditional board games, such as backgammon and chess, placed amongst the more practical items. Resonating with the window shoppers, these objects appear like relics from another era of economic stability and social mobility, offered here as props to evoke romantic images of mid-century leisure time.

There are several notices around the shop with pleas for donations of good quality second-hand and nearly-new goods. Unwanted furniture, in good condition, is particularly desirable, as well as kitchen items, paintings, small electrical items, silverware and ornaments. These are clearly the goods from which the shop is making the best profits. Martlets has a ready source of choice items of furniture, from the charity's warehouse furniture showrooms in Hove and Peacehaven.

It is essential for the shop to have a 'reserve' facility for its goods, because of its location. The road in front is closed, for the most part, to public traffic and the shop must find ways to facilitate customers' commitment to a sale, particularly if they must arrange transport. A sofa, with a 'Reserved' notice on the seat, has propped up on its cushions several framed prints that depict classic subjects such as flowers and country landscapes, as well as one drawing of the Brighton College building. Some of the more attractive frames appear to be moderately damaged but this just makes them look more authentic.

The cumbersome items are the most difficult to stock, in terms of removals and space, but they often fetch the highest prices, which are met more easily in the high street branches than in the warehouse. One volunteer tells me that, 'To a certain extent size is equitable with value, but, when space is at a premium, something like a piano is harder to shift, unless it is a particularly attractive one. Dining tables, chairs and sofas still sell consistently well because young couples need to find ways of saving money as they spend it, setting up home.' Her comment reminds me of the Tesco slogan, 'Helping You To Spend Less', and it occurs to me that the modern charity shop markets itself cannily on this principle as well. Charity shoppers may well complain in

general about the high prices of the more ambitious fundraising ventures but as long as it offers some saving the charity shop will always encourage liberal expenditure.

On a dining table (£165) next to the sofa (£85) there are neat stacks of china dinner services and cut-glass bowls. A classic wooden clotheshorse, laden with starched white lace and embroidered linen, gives the scene an antique appearance. A large wicker basket sits on the floor in the corner containing a collection of porcelain dolls that huddle together, dressed in Victorian children's garb. On a larger scale, tasteful women's outfits have been coordinated on a few mannequins that stand around the shop. At the back, the volunteer has just finished organising the clothes and ladies' shoes. Eveningwear, dinner suits and jewellery are also big sellers here, she tells me.

Ceramic and glass ornaments look content in their polished glass display cabinet with mirrored back. Full sets of drinks cabinet glasses are lined up beautifully in rows from the front to the back of the shelves. There are plenty of popular collectables such as commemorative Royal Family china and the nostalgic give-away memorabilia of time-honoured brands. Polished silverware, romantic trinkets and gifts for 'special occasions' line the bottom shelves and, under directed spotlights, the cabinet unit becomes a showcase of popular treasures.

In addition to its donated goods the shop also stocks a range of brand new goods, including balls of knitting wool, greeting cards, fashion jewellery, jams and biscuits. The wool is available in a range of attractive shades and is proving to be increasingly popular as fashion revisits traditional home crafts.

ADDRESS 150 North St. Brighton BN1 1RE TELEPHONE 01273 730 606 OPEN Monday to Saturday 10:15am - 5pm

Yesterdays, Katharine House Hospice - Stone, Staffordshire

Katharine House Hospice provides a range of services offering help, care and support for people with advanced life-limiting conditions across mid-Staffordshire. All services are free of charge.

Staffordshire has been called 'The Creative County' because of its history of creative and co-operative industry, and is especially known for its pottery towns in North Staffordshire. Stone is a spruce canal town just seven miles south of Stoke-on-Trent.

China and ceramics dominate the goods for sale in the 'Yesterdays' shop on Stone high street. A volunteer in the shop tells me that the retail staff are sent regularly on 'familiarisation' courses but that, through working at the shop, they soon become proficient in recognising the characteristic marks or properties of the different types of goods that come in, and distinguishing their common value. She was brought up in the Potteries and has an instinctive interest in the historic local product. She picks up a piece of china from the shelves, identifying its age and the pottery factory in which it was manufactured. There is plenty of Royal Doulton, Prince Albert, Copeland and Wedgwood china on display. She goes on to show me the bottom of a tea cup and saucer; 'If it just says "England' and not "made in...", it's usually pre-1920s,' she informs me. The value of a ceramic depends primarily on what colours are currently in fashion, how old the piece is and whether it is accompanied by its complete set. Branded earthenware continues to be highly collectable and there are many collectors' clubs looking out for the most rare and interesting examples. Despite competition amongst collectors in the search for the most desirable artefacts, plenty remain in circulation, despite dramatically reduced production in the UK in recent years, with many of the larger pottery plants closing as companies outsource work to the Far East.

Every two weeks Yesterdays rotates its stock around nine other Katharine House shops in the area. I ask if goods have often been noticed coming back. 'Very rarely!' is the answer. 'It's so surprising how much stock we get and it all goes out again,' she continues, describing the tidal nature of charity shops. In their book *Charity Shops: Retailing Consumption and Society*, Suzanne Horne and Avril Maddrell quote Margaret Atwood's *Lady Oracle*: 'What amazed me was the sheer volume of objects, remnants of lives and the way they circulated. The people died but their possessions did not, they went around and around in a slow eddy...' Goods are donated to the shops on a daily basis, they go out and something reliably different comes in to replace them.

The volunteer assistant used to work for one of the national charity shop chains but she tells me that she could not abide the amount of money that was spent on the London headquarters and paid management. She is much happier working for a local charity. 'Customers are more aware of where the money goes and understand that our *raison d'etre* is fundraising.' Even so, she reports that customers sometimes complain about the prices. 'They say "that's a bit expensive for a charity shop", but sadly they're missing the point. Why won't they pay the true value of something? If they want it, they want it!' she exclaims. She chooses to offer a comparative pricing example of an item of luxury goods – a gold necklace worth about £150 that the shop would sell for £100 - £125 – to illustrate how closely aligned the charity prices are with the market value of newly manufactured goods, in order to make the maximum amount of money for the charity. I can see it from her point of view but I am standing on the other side of the counter and my primary sympathy rests with the consumer, who not only takes pleasure in shopping as a pastime but, as part of this activity, appreciates the opportunity for thrift. The prices do not appear to deter customers, however, as the staff at the till are soon caught up in dealing with several purchases, indicating that this is a lucrative enterprise. Since the first shop opened ten years ago in Penkridge, the Hospice shops have raised over £2m.

Also on the local high street there is a Donna Louise Trust shop, along with a Cancer Research and Help The Aged.

ADDRESS 13 High Street, Stone, Staffordshire ST15 8AJ TELEPHONE 01785 816 907 OPEN Monday to Saturday 9:15am - 4:45pm

Hospices of Hope - Otford, Kent

Hospices of Hope are dedicated to improving the life of
the terminally ill in Romania and surrounding countries by
increasing access to hospice care and training.

Otford is a small Kent village, perversely inaccessible from the M25 motorway
beside which it nestles. This is a well-preserved and wealthy enclave of the
Home Counties, yielding ideal patrons for the Hospices of Hope's specialist
antiques shop and the award-winning tearooms opposite (see 'Tearooms'). The
tearooms is the smaller and original of the two shops, and once accommodated
the charity's head office upstairs, but headquarters have now moved across the
road to the larger outlet, which has expanded the charity's retail scope to add
a significant proportion to its income. This specialist initiative, focusing on
antiques and collectables, was set up in order to capitalise on a consistent influx
of valuable donations from local residents alongside the staff's growing interest
and expertise in this field of business.

A regular, commercial antiques shop occupies the remaining two retail
units next door. Otford Antique and Collectors' Centre is painted the same
racing-green and only a difference in the stencilled gold font of the shop
signage distinguishes the two enterprises. Together the shops command an
entire building on the high street, dedicated to antiques. Customers naturally
browse between the two. The Collectors' Centre offers advice on the value of
the charity's donations. If a customer is unable to sell an item next door they
are directed on to the charity shop. Although it is accepted that the Hospices'
prices are necessarily cheaper than its neighbour, it must be careful to maintain
the delicate symbiosis between non-profit and for-profit interests.

Unlike most shops that distinguish themselves with an antiques content,
this charity outlet has many collectable pieces of furniture through to small
items of bric-a-brac, and the quality resonates throughout. Although the shop
receives sufficient public donations, a continued effort is made to sustain the
standard by regularly supplementing stock, buying pieces to sell on at a profit
from the biannual Antiques and Collectors' Fair, which is held at the Memorial
Hall further down the road.

Prices are determined by fluctuating fashions and collectability at any
particular time. Some goods are more stable than others, secured in value by
brand as well as age, with only their condition and decorative design moderately
affecting price. A pair of Royal Doulton vases safely commands a price of £40.
A 1800s Wedgwood presentation plate costs £45 and a well-crafted Burleigh
coffee set is £65. Equally desirable is a 1950s Denbeigh bowl and a Glyn
Colledge cut crystal piece, priced similarly.

This shop freely caters to the romantic aesthetic of traditional tastes.
Victorian lace christening smocks hang close by a large porcelain doll. Lace
and crochet pieces cost around £5 each. Framed paintings and prints cover
the walls around the shop, on classic themes; sailing, arranged flowers and
country landscapes. Handsome examples of oil burning lamps and candle-

holders range from £10 to £55.

This is an immaculately presented shop that houses many articles, but feels remarkably uncluttered. The walls are clad with white tongue-and-groove wood panelling and a fitted oatmeal brown carpet creates a neutral, tasteful backdrop for the items on sale. Two rows of discrete glass shelves are suspended across the wide front window. Standing lamps and table lamps provide ancillary lighting and give a warm, homely context for the merchandise. Furniture creates a tableau of a formal household with various categories of ceramics and bric-a-brac arranged around it. An embroidered drawstring vanity bag hangs from the mirror fixing of a dressing-table. Dishes and ornamental pots sit on top, casually holding jewellery and other personal effects as they would in a boudoir bedroom. Side tables are laden with tea sets and a corner cabinet with vases and ornamental plates. A Victorian wash jug and basin sits on a carved oak plinth and a walnut-veneer table nest slips in beside it, discretely priced at £30.

To identify some of the smaller items within the furniture sets, some historical speculation is required. An Edwardian upholstered chair tucks neatly underneath a traditional writing desk with a leather inlay top on which sits an oil-burning lamp, a dye stamp and a box of graduated postage weights. Several vintage Bakelite fountain pens in their original boxes are fanned out across a matching side table, including a particularly attractive Conway Stewart model, for £20. A spot lit glass display cabinet contains smaller ceramic ornaments, jugs and teapots. There are fun items as well; old-fashioned branded tins, theatre programmes, opera glasses and tourist stationery from the post-war era. Boxes of traditional Variety matches are £1. Cast-iron cistern brackets add an unusual element of architectural salvage. The overall effect of the merchandise reflects the kind of considered eclecticism found in the grandest of English country homes.

ADDRESS 28 High Street (opposite Hospices of Hope Tearooms), Otford, Kent TN14 5PQ TELEPHONE 01959 525 110 OPEN Monday to Saturday 9:30am - 4:30pm

Hospice In The Weald - Cranbrook, Kent

The Hospice in the Weald is a seventeen-bed 'inpatient' unit that was established in 1980 as a home care service.

In 2002 the Hospice in the Weald opened its first specialist shop in Cranbrook selling antiques and collectables. There are now two Hospice shops in Cranbrook, the third – a small specialist bookshop in one of the Georgian terraced units further down Stone Street – is now closed, having been absorbed by the larger of the other two shops. The smaller shop remains a traditional charity shop, on the corner with High Street, selling the usual array of clothes and bric-a-brac.

The larger conglomerate shop is a more modern building that used to be a car garage, selling furniture, predominantly. The main body of the shop is filled with good quality sofas, crafted furniture and soft furnishings. Every piece in here is a stylish example of its kind, from antique veneer display cases and drinks cabinets (£45 to £60) to 1960s melamine-topped drop-leaf tables (around £15). Although the contemporary furniture effectively demonstrates its ergonomic design in this environment, the more cumbersome pieces still sell here at a premium because people in the locality have the space to house them and harbour a taste for a traditional aesthetic.

Reproductions of paintings hang closely together on the walls in frames, as well as a few original amateur artworks. Single drape samples of curtains provide a sumptuous backdrop for the furniture on the floor.

To the right lies a smaller room that now houses the bookshop collection, with a round table and chairs where customers can sit and browse the titles at leisure. Dried flowers in vases decorate a reproduction period dresser appropriated as a bookcase and daylight filters into the room from a single rear window. The books are mostly hardback copies, simply organised by category into fiction and non-fiction titles.

At the back of the shop the tables on sale are laid with full sets of crockery and cutlery. Again, traditional English Potteries china, such as Wedgwood, is displayed alongside retro sets. A long sideboard is neatly dressed with a pale pink and cream striped fabric, laden with highly collectable ceramic pieces and glassware. Carlton presentation plates line the shelves of a 1960s sideboard and wall-mounted shelves at the back, selling for between £5 and £10. The contrast and combination of periods works well together. A Victorian convex mirror hangs from the white-washed brick wall behind, to stylish effect.

There is also a decent spread of layers of starched and pressed table linen. A lot of the pieces are stained or moderately damaged but retain their appeal, embellished with handcrafted embroidery and personalised emblems.

The very back room has been turned into an office where the two joint managers sit, speaking on the phones, organising pick-ups and drop-offs for the shop.

ADDRESS Hospice In The Weald, Stone Street, Cranbrook Kent TN17 3HE
TELEPHONE 01580 714 538 OPEN Monday to Saturday 10am - 4pm, except Wednesday 10am - 1pm

Miscellenous crockery and homeware at Greenwich & Bexley Cottage Hospice, Welling ADDRESS 91 Bellegrove Road, Welling DA16 3PG TELEPHONE 020 8303 6864 OPEN Mondsy to Friday 10am - 4 pm

The Lothian Cat Rescue charity shop is the main fundraiser for the shelter. Popular amongst the city's keen charity shoppers because it has been preserved in its original manifestation with a cheaply-priced hotch-potch of donated goods, its large window display full of cat-themed ornaments and bric-a-brac is particularly interesting to collectors of cat memorabilia. The charity also holds monthly bazaars. ADDRESS 23 Easter Road, Edinburgh EH7 5PJ TELEPHONE 0131 661 3411 OPEN Monday to Saturday 10am - 4pm.

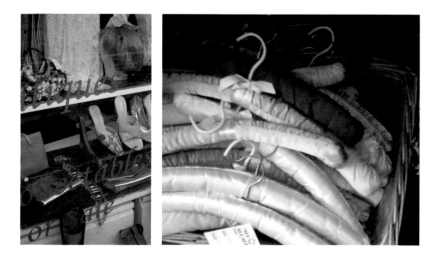

Padded hangers and window display at All Aboard, Swiss Cottage ADDRESS 150 Finchley Road, London NW3 5HS TELEPHONE 020 7431 3849 OPEN Monday to Friday 8.45am - 5pm

Buttons, wool and a decorative teapot at Queenscourt Hospice, Southport. With the help of a Townscape Heritage Initiative grant, the hospice has managed to replicate the original design of the traditional shop front. ADDRESS 15-19, Bold Street, Southport, Merseyside PR9 0DB TELEPHONE 01704 535 276 OPEN Monday to Saturday 10am - 4pm

Identifying 'collectables' at Faith Hope and Charity Shop, Christ Church. ADDRESS The Broadway, Totland Bay, Isle of Wight, PO39 0AT TELEPHONE 01983 752 031 (There is no phone at the shop, this is the church charity office number.) OPEN Monday to Saturday 10am - 4pm

Merchandise at Hospices of Hope, Otford, Kent (see page 60).

Ceramics at Hospice in the Weald, Cranbrook (see page 62).

Recently refurbished, St. Columba's Hospice, Morningside has a room at the back that is stocked with choice pieces of china and glassware. ADDRESS 195/7 Morningside Road, Edinburgh EH10 4QP TELEPHONE 0131 447 8686 OPEN Monday to Saturday 10am - 4pm

Tins and jars at Chelsea Oxfam Shop. ADDRESS 432 Kings Road, London SW10 OLJ TELEPHONE 020 7351 6863 OPEN Monday to Saturday 10:30am - 6:30pm

Dolls on display at the Royal Manchester Children's Hospital, Prestiwch. As part of the Five Stars Scanner Appeal, the Royal Manchester Children's Hospital has two shops located in Prestwich Village, currently aiming for a £1 million target. This shop resides nearby to the Longfield Centre with its concentration of charity shops. ADDRESS 446 Bury New Road, Prestwich, Manchester M25 1AZ TELEPHONE 0161 798 8754 OPEN Monday to Friday 9:30am - 4:30pm, Saturday 10am - 4pm

BOOKS, MUSIC & FILM

Age Concern @ 183 - Cowley Road, Oxford

Age Concern's mission is to promote the well-being of all older people and to help make later life a fulfilling and enjoyable experience.

As specialist shops go this Age Concern attracts immediate attention, having reinvented itself as a bookshop and Internet café that caters to the student population of the Cowley Road in the South Eastern district of Oxford. The shop is situated opposite the Carling live music venue that used to be called The Zodiac – an Oxon landmark of the alternative music scene since 1995.

The charity shop uses the abbreviated and symbol-drenched syntax of the computer age, incorporating the '@' sign in its fascia signage, to make itself instantly recognisable as an Internet facility. Identifying a gap in the market and acknowledging how vital Internet access is to the local student culture, it offers free WiFi with a single café purchase.

The walls throughout are painted a tomato red colour and, combined with a faux pine laminate floor, the interior has an atmosphere somewhere between fire-lit study and strip-lit office. In fact, natural daylight floods the Internet room at the back of the shop, through a large rear window. Framed art by local artists hangs on the walls, all for sale at prices hovering around the £200 mark. Three flat-screen computers and angle-poise lamps sit on the desktop stretching along one wall and comfortable leatherette office chairs encourage visitors to take their time online.

Free membership is offered to customers who then pay 90p for the first hour of Internet access and 30p for each fifteen minutes after that. Black and white printing is 9p per page and there is a minimum charge of £1. Those who choose to remain non-members pay a nominal ten per cent tax on prices. This pricing system seems a bit fussy but it is essentially generous and aims only to encourage regular use by offering benefits to members.

Members also enjoy a discount on café purchases. Refreshments are reasonably priced; a laminated pricelist on the wall offers (Fair Trade) Americano coffee for £1.30 and tea for £1. Soft drinks are also £1 and there are plenty of snack foods in the way of confectionary and crisps. Customers can help themselves to hot drinks, in a very relaxed and trusting set-up.

Separated from the back room by a few steps leading down into the main shop is the bookshop. There are a few small round tables at which to sit and read with a coffee as well as a more comfortable sofa in the front window where, on a clear day, customers can enjoy the warmth of the morning sunshine. The main shop floor is dedicated to books shelved by category – including all the sections that a customer might expect to find, despite the small scale of the operation. The art section is particularly comprehensive. On display is an immaculate hardback copy of *Goodbye Picasso* by David Douglas Duncan for £35, which strikes me as expensive, although this reflects its lack

of availability in mainstream shops.

There is a large bookcase in the rear corner selling '1st Editions, Signed Copies and Other Special' books. Many of these individual copies are also available through the charity's Amazon UK online account where I later look for an indication of comparative prices. The particularly desirable titles appear to be selling for about half of the market prices.

Charity bookshops commonly incorporate an audio visual section and so, to make up for this exclusion at Age Concern@183, I seek out a branch of Oxfam, further up the Cowley Road., towards the city centre, that sells a particularly good selection of records. Killing Joke's Revelations is a rare find at £3.99. I stock up on classic album cassette tapes, such as Depeche Mode's *Speak and Spell* and Frankie Goes To Hollywood's *Welcome to the Pleasuredome*. VHS films include several of the more obscure titles by Woody Allen. This shop too has a fairly extensive and well-researched book section and, for shoppers in the area, it is worth a look.

ADDRESS 183 Cowley Road, Oxford OX4 1UT TELEPHONE 01865 251 539
OPEN Monday to Saturday 10am - 6pm, Saturday 11am - 5pm.

Oxfam Bookshop - Durham, County Durham

Oxfam is an international development agency that helps
to put poor people in charge of their lives and livelihoods,
campaigning for change that lasts.

Oxfam is the largest retailer of second-hand books in Europe, selling around
eleven million books every year. Most of the seven hundred and fifty Oxfam
shops around Britain sell books and around one hundred of these are
specialist bookshops or book and music shops. Books are donated directly to
shops by the public, or through more than one thousand Oxfam book and
music banks in locations around the country. On a central level, books are
managed by the Bookbarn, which is a new wing of the Oxfam corporation,
sharing an industrial park site with its Wastesaver depot, in Leeds. The
Bookbarn aims to provide an internal recycling facility for Oxfam bookshops,
as well as operating as a prominent dealer in second-hand and antiquarian
books on an international scale, using both its recognised charity identity and
private company guises.

Durham's Oxfam Bookshop is one exemplary branch of the charity's
specialist shops. It is a traditional terraced building on Bridge Street. Away
from Elvert Bridge and the Boutique shop (see 'Boutique'), the Bookshop
offers its customers three floors of carefully selected books and includes a
music department on the top floor. The bookshop has been organised to
make the most of its shape and size. It is set out so that all the general and
weekend trade is contained within the ground and first floor areas, for
efficiency and comfort as well as security. Closed-circuit cameras send pictures
from all three floors to the front desk, reflecting the inevitable vulnerability
of such a large and segregated retail space, but staff members are unobtrusive
in their presence as guardians on the shop floor.

There is a wide selection of modern fiction and leisure interest titles, a large
classics section and several rare or collectable books, including a first edition
from Agatha Christie. The fiction section is divided into science fiction and
crime and general titles under an A to Z of authors. Many of the books are
in the 'Top 40' listing. On the ground floor there is also space allocated to
Oxfam's Fairtrade foods and Change range. There is a good selection of greeting
cards, recycled and environmentally friendly products. During the run up to
Christmas this selection swells to include Oxfam Christmas cards, calendars
and diaries, from which the charity secures a substantial annual profit.

Stained wooden floorboards and bespoke bookcases, including one large
carved wooden centrepiece bookcase on the ground floor, is all that is required
in addition to the standard bracketed shelving to give a feel of authority
and grandeur to the shop. The refurbished staircase remains a characterful,
creaky climb to the first floor non-fiction room. A fireplace stacked with
wood, built-in shelving on either side of the chimney breast and a framed
landscape painting above the mantelpiece are a homely focus point to the

room. Upholstered armchairs in traditional fabrics and a red leather footstool create a relaxed, domestic setting in which to sit and read the books on travel, gardening, cookery, natural history, humour and biographical writing.

The shop specialises in academic books to cater for the needs of the university students and many have commented on the savings they have been able to make on purchases for their reading lists. Specialist stock, which also includes music titles and recordings, is kept on the top floor, where two deep-seated, jacquard sofas offer further comfortable seating to browsing customers. Table lamps with clean cream shades sit on the windowsill and more shelving has been built up in front. The academic room comprises religion, law, politics, economics, social science and history. The quality of the books and the condition of the book jackets are impeccable.

The music room at the back of the building houses an immaculate display of recorded and written music, styled by a gramophone prop and gleaming showcase cabinet full of vintage audio equipment. Thousands of CDs, DVDs, story tapes and sheet music books are densely packed together over the expanse of the wall and a large and growing collection of vinyl records are contained neatly in uniform black wooden boxes around waist-height shelves.

For the moment Oxfam Durham does not sell on eBay but it hopes to do so in the future. The two specialist shops, overseen by one manager, require volunteers to help to set this up. There is currently a core team of around thirty people that increases to around fifty when the students return after the summer, but Internet auction sales are labour-intensive and require the sustained and focused effort of a handful of people. Any high-value books go on sale in the shop. 'We feel it is very important that both donors and customers see that we can and do sell valuable books. We find that like attracts like with all donations,' says the manager.

ADDRESS 12 Elvet Bridge, Durham DH1 3AA TELEPHONE 0191 384 6366 OPEN Monday to Sunday 10am - 5pm.

Books Etcetera, Shakespeare Hospice - Stratford, Warwickshire

Shakespeare Hospice is an independent local charity providing specialist palliative day care for people living in the Stratford-upon-Avon district, living with a life-limiting illness.

This shop was launched in March 2008, to handle the overwhelming amount of books donated by the Stratford community to the Shakespeare Hospice. Situated in Rother Street, in the town centre, Books Etcetera is the first specialist charity bookshop to arrive in the region. It sells predominantly second-hand books and, as the second half of the shop title suggests, it also stocks a further range of goods, in the form of recorded music, printed sheet music, films and computer-game software.

The deep, carpet-covered shelf in the window of the shop does little to attract the attention of the passer-by but instead faces inwards, offering bargain books in a series of cardboard boxes – all priced at £1. Facing the counter and at the other end of the pricing spectrum is the 'Antiques and Collectables' section, advertising most prominently twelve hardback volumes of Proust's *Remembrance of Things Past,* at a price marked down from £20 to £10. The rest of the bookshop is made up of freestanding shelf units, dividing the non-fiction books into category and the fiction titles by author.

There are signed copies of books behind the counter and the most expensive records sit on display shelves alongside them. The Beatles' *Red Album* is £30. There are two further rooms towards the back of the shop and security cameras continuously transmit a series of rough images of the shop floor to the front desk.

The middle section of the shop has a different feel. There are a few collections of back-copy magazines stacked in piles. An odd louvre blind rests upright against the wall in its original but tatty sheath packet. I see that the eclectic medley of songs playing on the compact stereo on the floor is a hoard of free compilation CDs labelled, 'Freebies to play for background music'.

The back room is full of music of all kinds. A large display unit occupies the centre of the space and houses LPs on one side and CDs, cassette tapes, DVDs, VHS videos and computer games on the other. A printed pricelist is tacked to the wall; all albums are £1 and singles are 50p, unless otherwise marked. I am happy to see that taped media is still worthy of sale rather than scrap, despite fetching only a nominal amount. There are even several TDK 90 blank, recordable cassette tapes on offer for 25p, which I buy for my dictaphone.

The walls are sparsely decorated with a few paintings and framed posters, each of them for sale. An *Empire Strikes Back* poster hints at the generation that the shop imagines most of its collectors to belong to. A table and chairs are placed invitingly next to wall-mounted shelves of books. A Pete Doherty biography is boldly displayed alongside Francoise Hardy and Supergrass records, for £10, £8 and £20 respectively. There are plenty of 78s and a dedicated '70s/80s Soul' section, for alternative interests, all contained in

colourful plastic storage boxes on the floor. Box-sets have their own hand-labelled section.

Jethro Tull seems to have once been popular, with several discarded albums in the collection here, and so I take a chance on two early albums at £2 each. An immaculate 12" New Order single is £1 and Kraftwerk's *Trans Europe Express* is £3. The records in this charity shop tempt me to duplicate my entire record collection, amassed since teenage-hood. At this particular moment, I fight the urge to double-up on well-preserved copies of classic and much-loved albums such as Wings' *Greatest Hits*, Supertramp's *Even In The Quietest Moments* or Depeche Mode's *Speak & Spell*. Good-quality vinyl sells as both a fetish object and a historical document, justified by its investment value. More often than not, when I come across a record and cannot remember if I already own it, I play it safe and buy it.

An older male volunteer sees that I have *Songs From A Room* by Leonard Cohen tucked under my arm and he promptly disappears upstairs, reappearing with a copy of *Songs Of Love And Hate* to offer me in addition. Unfortunately I already have this album, I explain, and I am buying a copy of the other to replace one that disappeared recently from my collection. Overall, the LPs here are far superior to the usual charity shop stock, and are not overwhelmed by the familiar bestselling editions of rock and pop titles.

This is one of five Shakespeare Hospice shops. There is another, of the more traditional kind, nearby on Greenhill Street. The charity's warehouse shop is located at Burton Farm, just outside the town, towards Warwick.

ADDRESS 43 Rother Street, Stratford-upon-Avon, Warwickshire CV37 6LP TELEPHONE 01789 209 232 OPEN Monday to Friday 9:30am - 4:30pm, Sunday 9:30am - 4pm

Demelza, Demelza House Hospice - Herne Bay, Kent

Demelza House is the only children's residential hospice for inhabitants of Kent, East Sussex and South London, providing one-to-one care and a wide range of services to life-limited children.

There is a fluctuating total of around thirteen charity shops in the small seaside town of Herne Bay and this is one of two Demelza House Hospice shops currently in operation. The other, on William Street, is a traditional charity shop but five minutes walk up Mortimer Street and close to the high street resides this specialist bookshop. It opened to provide relief for the original shop on popular book donations and enables the charity to capitalise on this significant portion of its stock. By separating books, essentially into the realm of luxury item, the charity is able to achieve better prices and dramatically increase turnover on the bulk. The inception of a second-hand charity bookshop in Herne Bay has also addressed the need for affordable books in a low-income area. There is currently only one other bookshop in the town, selling new books to a niche audience, and the two businesses have not yet initiated a relationship.

Demelza occupies a listed building on Mortimer Street – the old 'wagon road' through the town – at the corner with Chapel Street. The unit is thought to be the first shop in Herne Bay and the charity proudly advertises its place in history, in a printed online article in the window. The shop opened as a grocer's and off-license at the beginning of the 20th century and the youngest daughter of the greengrocer still lives above the shop. The grocery shop finally closed in 1974 and, although it has changed function several times since, operating as a china shop latterly, the weather-boarded building stands virtually unaltered today.

Inside, the shop has retained its original dark, oak wood shelving units that run in grid formation from floor to ceiling, in the smaller, sheltered part of the interior that it shares with the till-counter on the left side. The carpeted floor and its effect on the acoustics of the room add to the tenebrous setting, akin to the intimacy of a library. The books are organised alphabetically and the shelves here are dedicated to fiction titles, which sell best. The brighter and more spacious region of the shop, on the right side, looking out through a long stretch of window on to the street, appears fractionally more contemporary and yet conventional, stocking the non-fiction titles as well as children's literature.

Eddie Walker has thirty years experience in book sales and now helps to run the shop – staffed entirely by volunteers – four days a week. He is aware that the price for which he can sell a book in the locality may be much less than its market value. He feels that high street 'specialists' tend to overprice, particularly in today's diversified market, and it is important not to keep

dead stock that does not sell. To its advantage, the shop is able to rotate some of its books with another Demelza House bookshop further east along the coast in Hythe. Eddie describes this shop, in contrast, as modish and attributes its polish to the generally wealthier community that it serves. He tells me a rumour about another regional charity shop that recently received a first edition James Bond book, which has sparked the imaginations of the enthusiasts and collectors amongst the Herne Bay community. He says that his customers are always looking out for the next popular classic, citing the Robert Markham *Colonel Sun* novel as an example.

The shop has a small collection of collectables and first editions, behind the counter. The last second-hand and antiquarian bookseller in the town closed down three years ago but he continues to offer free advice and valuations to the Demelza shop. Eddie has considered auctioning these books online but he does not have the time himself or the manpower to set up the operation. As far as I can see, there is no need to speed up the revolution in this quietly successful establishment. The prices are gauged to suit the needs of the locale. Whilst it is important not to price donations too low unwittingly, Eddie believes that it is far more important not to overprice the books, so as not to alienate potential customers. As well the practical motivations, there is an ethical dimension to his approach. 'The shop might not achieve the top prices but a cheap book promotes reading,' Eddie points out. 'If it costs nothing in the first place then why hang on to it for a few extra pounds?' he says.

ADDRESS 165 Mortimer Street, Herne Bay CT6 5HE TELEPHONE 01227 283 806 OPEN Monday to Saturday 9:30am - 4:30pm

Treetops Hospice Bookshop - Eastwood, Nottinghamshire

Treetops Hospice aims to help people with life-limiting illnesses such as cancer, multiple sclerosis and motor neurone disease achieve the best quality of life possible.

Eastwood is a former coalmining town in the Broxtowe district, on the border between two counties, Derbyshire and Nottinghamshire. Its distinct red sandstone terraced houses constructed around the high street on Nottingham Road look out high up over the nearby metropolises. Author D.H. Lawrence was born in Eastwood. His birthplace and residences now attract visitors from all over the world. Many of his best-known novels describe Eastwood and its culture, and among his works are poems written in the local dialect.

The Treetops Hospice bookshop is positioned on a mainly residential street that runs perpendicular to the end of the high street. It nevertheless enjoys a good level of passing trade from customers en route to Nottingham Road from the free car park around the corner. The shop's small front window is stacked with greeting cards and large-format game and craft books. Inside, two small adjoining rooms constitute the main body of retail space. As I walk in through the door I see straight ahead of me a 'classic titles' section. Searching first for a book by D.H. Lawrence I find a Cambridge University Press edition of *Lady Chatterley's Lover*. Many popular titles are present here in paperback form, including modern and 20th century classics. There are several interesting Critical Editions' educational reference books, some hardback Sherlock Holmes' novels and a tooled, gold-leaf Reader's Digest volume. There are also several children's classics, set low on the shelves, such as Rupert the Bear annuals, which bear images that immediately conjure rousing emotions from my childhood.

A volunteer sits behind the till at the front of the shop, sunk into the piles of books that surround her. A walnut-effect laminate plastic coats the front of the glass counter to a surprisingly quaint effect. Bare brick walls, painted white against bold green woodwork, lend a simple, romantic power to this intimate library setting. Books are piled on the shelves in a tumbledown fashion. Further categories in this part of the shop include travel (with a large selection of out-of-date guides, atlases and maps), reference, lifestyle and poetry books. 'Barb's Cards' is a selection of handmade greeting cards that have been made by local resident and volunteer, Barbara, who donates her craftwork to the shop for a small return on the profits.

In the back of the shop, fiction writers are catalogued from 'A' to 'Z'. The major themes are 'crime writing' and 'romantic fiction'. I decide to read, for the first time, an Inspector Rebus novel by Ian Rankin called *The Hanging Garden*, named after a Cure song, which costs me £1. A wicker basket on the table occupying the centre of the room contains a small collection of records, each valued at roughly the same price. All cassette tapes and CDs are offered at the end of the bookshelves for 50p. I ask the volunteer if there is a pricing system that staff adhere to, and how the particularly low prices that I have noticed can possibly cover overheads. She tells me that most of the volunteers are committed to working a minimum of one four-hour shift each week and, whilst some do more, that single shift does not enable staff to sustain any definite pricing plan or familiarise themselves with the stock. She continues to notice, however, that between her shifts the titles do change, which suggests that the prices manage to keep the stock moving.

Treetops Hospice also transfers a lot of stock through car boot sales, in season. In addition to its book specialism, the charity is currently calling for a public 'Wedding Dress Amnesty', motivated by the idea of holding a fundraising sale at a prestigious local venue that will be lent free of charge for the occasion. Everyone who donates dresses will play a vital role in amassing the stock required to open a charity bridal shop at a later date. Nearby, the Giltbrook retail park is undergoing a £60 million expansion, due to be completed by Christmas 2008.

ADDRESS 7 Victoria Street, Eastwood, Nottinghamshire NG16 3AW TELEPHONE 01773 711 800 OPEN Monday, Tuesday, Thursday and Friday, 10am - 4pm, Wednesday and Saturday 10am - 1pm

St. John, Charity Books Plus - Stockbridge, Edinburgh

As well as the world-famous St John Ambulance Service, St. John supports Mountain Rescue in Scotland, eye-hospitals in the Middle East and helps with a number of other good causes throughout the UK and beyond.

Newly open after refurbishment, this outstanding specialist bookshop has been successfully rebranded Charity Books Plus and looks perfectly in keeping with any private antiquarian dealership. Full-time volunteer manager and avid book collector Robert Mullin tells me that the shop has already smashed last year's annual profits of £1,300, taking £1,500 in its first week of trading. The charity shop was previously run by elderly volunteers who simply did not have the energy levels needed to make the retail operation a profitable income for St John.

Under his management, Robert opened the larger back room to the public, instantly giving the shop a much higher turnover, currently stocking between eight and ten thousand books, from precious 19th century editions to brand new publications. There is a sizeable children's section in the back room, along with a collection of reference books in which all topics are covered, with only 'philosophy' currently underrepresented. There are books on interesting local subjects, including the city of Edinburgh itself and Fettes College that is

situated nearby. The shop also stocks CDs and DVDs, vinyl records, including 78s, maps, postcards, greeting cards, prints and a small amount of curiosity bric-a-brac.

In the main front room of the shop, there are several large bookcases containing the more interesting or valuable books. There are currently a few signed copies of John Buchan novels. A glass display cabinet proudly presents a series of seven vellucent bindings – hand-painted boards covered in vellum and stamped with mother of pearl. Signed and with a dedication, a book of Scottish colourist Francis Cadell, called *Tommy and Jack*, contains his loose watercolours of army life. Bonham's recently sold a copy, unsigned, for £799. The Portland Gallery in London, which handled Cadell's art at the time of his death, bid £850 on the book but was outbid by Robert's sister who bought it two years in advance of his fiftieth birthday for her partner, who became familiar with the artist coincidentally through playing bridge with his daughter. There are a lot of books here from the Golden Age of illustration, including works by Arthur Rackham and a book illustrated by a Glasgow School artist, Jessie M. King. The bookshop has an important collection for sale, valued at between £20,000 and £25,000.

A charity bookshop does not have the same clientele as an antiquarian dealer or auction house and the stock is priced accordingly. Before its official opening, the shop attracted local dealers who naturally came to investigate the competition and negotiate the purchase of some of the more noteworthy titles. Robert says that he is happy to price the books deliberately so that the dealers will buy them, in sharp contrast to the prevalent attitude amongst charity shop staff who block the cheap sale of items that may then be sold on for personal profit. He does not see an easy sale as a loss to the charity but a profit nevertheless and contributing to a more sustainable venture that incorporates the inevitable selfish interests of some of its customers.

There are no sales by the back door here. Robert feels strongly that presales on stock deny the public access to the more unique acquisitions. The books are competitively priced and their value carefully considered, and so bartering is prohibited. Books here are about half the cost of those at Oxfam, whose prices tend to be a standard point of comparison for other charity shops because they are able to set them high. The contrast conveys value for money at St. John.

Robert believes that the charity shop should aim to serve two purposes; to raise funds for a parent charity but also to provide cheaper goods for local communities. A charity shop can be a vital resource to the community in supporting itself by the redistribution of goods. A charity bookshop, however, has a slightly different ratio of responsibility to those charity shops selling essential items such as clothes or furniture, because books are considered to be a luxury item. The reasonable pricing at Charity Books Plus, therefore, is dictated by practicality rather than principle. The emergence of 'budget retail' provides a counterpoint to this view, whereby immediate need is satiated, and it is perhaps the role of the specialist charity shop to offer a unique opportunity to boost the general standard of living in its locale, with a higher calibre of cultural artefacts.

Stockbridge is, in fact, a particularly affluent area of Edinburgh. Some customers, Robert speculates, use the shop to look for books that they cannot find in a regular bookshop, such as out-of-print titles. He describes the element of surprise that the charity shop offers as an alternative to those mainstream shops in which the taxonomy is familiar and the stock is ubiquitously available: 'The majority of people come in to the shop looking for "odd" stuff. They don't necessarily know what they're looking for but they might take a fancy to something.'

Robert is passionate about the books that he sells and likes to talk to the customers, advising them and enlightening them on the various histories and particular features of his collection. He volunteers his expertise six days a week, making his own money through website design and writing, and finds working for a charity ultimately satisfying. 'At the moment, St. John is raising money for a travelling hospice in Malawi. People working for the bigger charities don't get to see the specific results of their fundraising efforts. At the end of the year I will be able to see exactly where our profits have gone, to buy an ambulance, for example,' he explains.

The shop is situated opposite the other charity shops of Stockbridge, on the side of the road that is controlled by strict parking regulations. Robert built up the current stock prior to the opening by writing to people for offerings. In order to achieve a target of £75,000 for the year, the shop needs to maintain its level of quality merchandise and Robert continues to be proactive in soliciting donations. Freecycle and Gumtree are useful websites for advertising and a website for the shop is under construction, to conduct online sales, giving exposure to the more valuable books so that their full value can be realised and so that the charity can continue to make money when foot-flow past the shop is slow. The shop has now been open for three months and, to date, £16,500 has been raised, £4000 of which has been realised through eBay sales. The charity's eBay account opened just over a month ago, which means that the shop made approximately £1000 a week from online sales.

St. John takes in all donations, regardless of quality. Less attractive books are put outside in a '50p' bin, which draws in customers. The shop has an ongoing deal with another local charity, The Edinburgh Furniture Initiative, which provides second-hand furniture for people setting themselves up in new tenancies. EFI receive a lot of books as part of their donations and it finds these to be most valuable as a cash exchange with St. John, which buys between ten and twenty boxes each week at a cost of £10 per box. By establishing a solid support and exchange network with other charities in the area, the charity shop can secure a reliable income of goods.

ADDRESS 20 Deanhaugh Street, Stockbridge, Edinburgh EH4 1LY TELEPHONE 0131 332 4911 OPEN Monday to Saturday 10am - 5pm, Sunday 12pm - 4pm

Lindsey Lodge Hopsice Shop, Scunthorpe. ADDRESS 289 Ashby High Street, Scunthorpe DN16 2RX TELEPHONE 01724 282 391 OPEN Monday to to Friday 9:30am - 4pm Saturday 9:30am - 1pm

Shop front at Animal Aid and Advice. ADDRESS 203, Blackstock Road, Highbury, London N5 211 TELEPHONE 020 7359 0294 OPEN Monday to Sunday 10am - 6pm

An orderly window display at Books and Things, Mind, Newcastle. ADDRESS 74 Clayton Street, Newcastle upon Tyne NE1 5PG TELEPHONE 0191 221 1540 OPEN Monday to Saturday 9:30am - 5pm, Sunday 11am - 4pm

Penguin classics and other collectable titles on display at Freshfields, Southport. ADDRESS 22-24 Wesley Street, Southport, Merseyside PR8 1BN TELEPHONE 01704 538 389 OPEN Monday to Saturday 9:30am - 5:30pm Except Thursday 9:30am - 4pm, Sunday 12pm - 4pm

Themed window displays at St. Catherine's Hospice Bookshop, Chorley. ADDRESS 54 Chapel Street, Chorley, Lancashire PR7 1BS TELEPHONE 01257 273 258 OPEN Monday to Saturday 10am - 4pm

St Giles Hospice Bookshop, Mere Green. ADDRESS 284a Lichfield Rd, Mere Green, Sutton Coldfield, West Midlands B74 2UG TELEPHONE 0121 308 0006 OPEN Monday to Saturday 9:15am - 4:30pm

Mounted record covers from St Gemma's Hospice Ilkley. ADDRESS 24 Brook Street, Ilkley, West Yorkshire LS29 8DE TELEPHONE 01943 817 150 OPEN Monday to Saturday 9am - 5pm, Sunday 11am - 4pm

Oxfam Music & Audio - Ealing Broadway, London

Oxfam is one of the most experienced development agencies in the world, now working in more than seventy countries. Providing help in an emergency often leads to long-term involvement with particular communities.

Almost all Oxfam shops sell CDs and vinyl but this specialist Music & Audio shop offers an even wider range of CDs, vinyl, sheet music and music books. A Maneki Neko beckoning cat is the shop's lucky mascot, greeting visitors from the main front window display. The showcase facing the street has a range of top merchandise. A Bang & Olufsen music centre with turntable and built-in tuner is priced competitively at £120. A portable Squire guitar amp hints at a stock of musical instruments inside. A *Classic ABBA* CD case is repeated for visual impact across the side wall of the display and this is juxtaposed with the LP sleeve of Boito's *Mefistofele*, depicting the devil from *Faust*.

At the end of a smart terrace of shops facing The Green is this relatively small commercial outlet unit, with grand proportions. A giant wooden reconstruction of the cover of The Beatles' *Sgt Pepper's Lonely Hearts Club Band* album dominates the tall space, signed by its designer, artist Sir Peter Blake, and insured by Oxfam for £4,000. A full Linko drum kit sits on the floor in the centre of the room, selling for £59, excluding hardware. The shop stocks four categories of music-related items. Vinyl, CDs, DVDs, videos and electrical audio equipment are all represented, in top-notch quality.

Playing on the stereo is a compilation of orchestral interpretations of famous rock songs. There are no classical records on sale because apparently they do not sell. The classical market has moved on to CD. Rock and pop commands the shelves here, in every format. Other categories are soul/R&B, dance, 12" singles, jazz/blues, reggae and 60s.

Vinyl occupies the length of one wall. Albums are displayed with their sleeves facing forward, giving an immediate impression of the type of selection available. The more valuable titles have been extracted and mounted on the wall above, to the effect of heightening expectations of a rare find. There is endless opportunity to back up a record collection with some reliable classics, for between £10 and £20 a piece. *Andy Warhol's Velvet Underground Featuring Nico*, Miles Davis' *Sketches of Spain* and Pink Floyd's *Dark Side of the Moon* are just a few examples on display.

The most collectable items that the shop receives in the way of donations are saved for sale on eBay, where by broadening its audience the shop can set the high prices that would otherwise have to be capped much lower in the charity shop. A signed copy of the recent Live Aid programme, signed by all four members of Pink Floyd and donated to the shop by the band's manager, recently sold at auction for over £5,000. A Beatles acetate (master copy) just came in with a donated personal collection, worth well over £1,000. Occasional sales of this kind go a long way to supporting the Ealing outlet.

Quality control is unsurpassably strict and every piece of vinyl appears to be in mint condition. The LPs provide most of the sales and the shop cannot afford to compromise its reputation by taking on lesser quality records. 'Most of our regulars do not even bother to check the condition of the vinyl and no one has returned anything in over two years,' asserts Oxfam. Every record is inspected for defects and if it is not up to standard then it is binned or passed on. The shop must pay for disposal and so it must be choosy about the donations that it accepts. It has invested in a machine to clean the records and remove static. Only the album sleeves are put out on the shelves. To prevent degradation through continuous handling and preserve their pristine condition the albums are kept behind the till counter in their inner sleeves, where the customer can check the state of the plastic at the point of purchase.

I buy *Hall of the Mountain Grill* by Hawkwind and the Kinks' *Lola* LP, for £7.99 and £4.99, suspecting that I am paying a premium. The shop claims an unrivalled status in offering the lowest prices possible for its merchandise, in terms of rarity and condition, and offers the supporting example of an original vinyl issue of a Jimmy Smith album that would cost £11.99 in this Oxfam, compared to around £25 elsewhere. If we are to accept this as a demonstration of the shop's pricing policy then the customer should expect to pay just under half the market value for any second-hand record.

Over the past few years the shop has become increasingly independent of the charity's headquarters and is now entirely responsible for acquiring its own stock. To boost donations, the shop has a set up a Gift Bank system, providing offices with branded cardboard deposit boxes for unwanted CDs. Many of the big record company offices have taken this on and radio stations and magazines give regularly in large quantities. CDs that sell for between £8 and £16 in most record shops average out at £2.99 here. There is a comprehensive back-catalogue of many of the artists as well as titles that are no longer available.

Several customers browse through the tightly packed spines of VHS videotapes and DVDs in the film section at the back of the shop, and I look past their shoulders at a wide range of titles that comprise mainly popular recent releases but also include a good selection of world cinema and Disney classics. There are several Tartan and BFI releases in the mix, costing around £7 each. The audio department is defined by a shallow cove of fragmented shelving that displays everything from retro to modern music systems, video and DVD players and television sets. Contemporary brands are known for being of the highest quality. A Quad amplifier is £160, and about half the online asking-price. Retro equipment, including gleaming Bakelite valve radios, appears to be in excellent condition. Everything is PAT-tested and checked over by resident expert David Russell to ensure Health and Safety standards are met and all sales come with a one-month warranty.

ADDRESS 23 The Green, Ealing, London W5 5DA TELEPHONE 020 8810 1932 OPEN Monday to Saturday 9:30am - 6pm, Sunday 10am - 5:30pm

Fircroft Trust - Surbiton, Surrey

The Fircroft Trust supports adults living in the community with mental health problems and/or learning disabilities and enables them to maximise their potential through positive action for mind and body. It provides care in four residential homes and through the services of a Centre.

This shop receives a lot of artwork, which is put up around the walls as decoration and to attract buyers. Also of particular appeal is the fact that it is one of just two charity shops in Surbiton that sells electrical goods. An electrician visits three days a week and each checked item normally sells within a day or two. Anything with a plug is tested with a Portable Appliance Tester and logged with a serial number to satisfy Trading Standards. The old hi-fi separates are popular and the shop recently put together a mix and match hi-fi composed of different brands that immediately sold for £100. Beauty appliances also sell remarkably quickly. To increase profits, there is a small room in the middle of the shop that is dedicated to books as well as a back room given over to clothing.

In the long, thin vestibule adjoining the main room, there is a small secondary front window and a feeble shelving unit that strains under the weight of records. Most of the vinyl that comes in to the shop is worth little more than £1 a piece but a couple of volunteers cross-reference anything that looks interesting in the donation bags and boxes with the Record Collectors' Guide to find any of higher value. Using its unique number the common value of a record is easily established and the rule of thumb here is to mark it at a quarter of the price, depending on the condition. If it is very valuable then it might be priced at as much as half the catalogue price. Of the vintage titles on offer, a Grateful Dead LP is £3, The Rolling Stones is £5 and The Beatles' *Sgt. Pepper's Lonely Hearts Club* and *Led Zeppelin I* are both £15, all reasonably priced in view of their collectability.

The front room of this charity shop is filled from floor to ceiling with bric-a-brac, including the front window, and a lot of the stock is considered to be collectable, with antique value. Manager Derryck Butcher does not extract goods to sell on eBay because he believes strongly that local customers should benefit from the higher quality donations. Guide prices are not used to value this category of goods, which is priced according to what staff feel is realistic. There is a 'win some, lose some' attitude as, although they are careful to maintain profits for the charity, the staff realise that pricing mistakes are inevitable. Derryck is candid about one recent oversight whereby the shop sold a Victorian fairing – a small porcelain ornament handed out at fairgrounds in the 19th century – for £2.50. Derryck noticed just as it was picked up by a customer, who said that she was a collector. To this day he is not sure if the lady knew its antique value was over £150.

In fact, the odd mistake is likely to make the shop more money in the long term than each underpriced sale because of the reputation that those oversights generate. 'If people do not feel they are getting the occasional bargain they won't come back,' says Derryck. Prices are deliberately designed to attract collectors, usually willing to spend more on the right item, and kept low enough to attract dealers to take a chance on an item, to sell on at a small profit if they so wish. It is also the intention that 'ordinary' customers should be able to afford to buy the goods they find and love.

The Surbiton shop is one of two Fircroft Trust shops. The other, in Tolworth, is a dedicated furniture shop, whilst Surbiton is an uncommonly varied shop due to the sheer quantity of donations that it receives and puts straight out on to the shop floor. The Fircroft Trust just recently sold forty die-cast model cars to one collector, having been uncertain as to whether they would sell at all and thus demonstrating the difficulties in predicting what will go on to make money for the charity. Outside, the shop even retains its common junk to sell on at bargain prices.

Derryck estimates that around sixty per cent of doorstep deposits come in a broken or un-saleable state, which he suspects are items that have been thrown away rather than donated. The shop seems often to be used as a dump in lieu of the local tip and this causes a problem with disposal of such goods, but it is simply accepted by Derryck as part of the mechanics of running a charity shop. The rest of the merchandise is an eclectic mix of the practical and the unusual. Customers often comment on how good the shop is for rummaging. I watch each person that comes through the door stand in one place for a while to take in the range of merchandise, seemingly determined not to miss anything. In this respect the shop retains the quaintness of the old-world charity shops.

'We fix the prices to be fair and yet we are always expected to knock down those prices,' says Derryck. 'We appreciate everything that is donated and in a sense it is free but it has been donated with the hope of raising money for the charity.' There is a sign saying 'Please do not ask for discount' on which Derryck comments, 'You wouldn't ask Sainsbury's for a discount. Our responsibility is to realise the value of our donations. If the shop makes a loss then it's breaking the charity's covenant and we can no longer operate as a Trading Company.' There are several other charities making an appearance along Surbiton high street and The Fircroft Trust sees the competition as helpful. There is a different ethos in each of the charity shops here, which is quite clear in their contents and the prices they charge. Derryck continues, 'For us its not a case of going for the top dollar all the time. As long as we continue to make a profit for the charity, everyone can benefit.'

ADDRESS 1a St Andrews Road, Surbiton, Surrey KT6 4DT TELEPHONE 0208 390 5597 OPEN Monday to Saturday 9:30am - 5:30pm

British Heart Foundation, Books & Music - Cheltenham, Gloucestershire

The BHF pioneers research into the causes of heart disease and improved methods of prevention, diagnosis and treatment.

Located just off the main pedestrian shopping street in historic Cheltenham is a British Heart Foundation shop dedicated to 'Books & Music'. This is one of six such operations initiated by the charity, which together boast a choice of over five thousand books and more than two thousand music-related items. There is a common pricing scheme for all the shops. Paperback fiction costs 50p a book and promotions offering three books for £2 encourage sales on a regular basis. Some thought has been given to the main occasions on which the public chooses to buy books, with promotions tailored to holiday times and summer titles. Last year the Books & Music shops sold over three million books and almost two million records, videos, cassettes and CDs.

Standing in front of the records it is immediately evident that there is a better than average selection of charity shop vinyl here. Music takes up most of the shop floor on a large central display unit. 12" records are stacked with their sleeves facing forwards, forfeiting premium space to the privilege of easy browsing. Despite the number of records, this shop is surprisingly uncluttered and a great proportion of the titles are at the popular end of the alternative spectrum. Those that have been pulled to the front include The Fall *A-Sides* for £1.99 and Talking Heads *Fear of Music* for £4.99. Deeper into the collection I flick past *Big Meaty Bouncy* by The Who, *Fried* by Julian Cope and *Tango in the Night* by Fleetwood Mac. The familiar appearance of Duran Duran contrasts with The Meteors, a psychobilly band whom I have never previously seen represented in a charity shop.

Considering the unusual titles available in this branch, a curious selection of records have been extracted for presentation on the wall. Records from Yazz and Human League are pinned up with several of the better known Bowie albums, all for £1.99 each. In the 7" singles section at the end of the row I pull out a copy of Supertramp's *Breakfast In America*. There are plenty of cassette tapes that may contribute finally to a fully comprehensive collection of music. The entire Aerosmith anthology is present in cassette format, amidst the more generic, popular one-timers. It is usual to find in a charity shop endless duplicates of platinum status albums that suggest the collection has been pre-sorted at different stages in its accumulation, prior to reaching the shelves. I long for evidence of personal collections and this particular grouping has an organic quality.

The charity boasts on its website some rare records recently 'found in (BHF) shops', which include Frank Zappa's *Freak Out*, The Rolling Stones'

High Tide and Green Grass, as well as an original mono pressing of *Their Satanic Majesties Request*. A first edition of a 1960s *Biggles* book has also been donated to a BHF shop.

Whilst the music section of the Cheltenham shop focuses customers' attention on the centre of the space, it is the array of books on shelves lining the walls that leads them around the room. There are plenty of hardback presentation books in the non-fiction categories, all at reasonable prices, with the art books achieving the highest prices. The fiction section delivers some unexpected and exciting titles, including Thomas Bernhard's *The Loser* and a copy of Harry Matthews' *Sinking of the Odradek Stadium*.

ADDRESS 25 Winchcombe Street, Cheltenham GL52 2LZ TELEPHONE 01242 222 425 OPEN Monday to Saturday 9am - 5pm

Oxfam - Broad Street, Oxford

Oxfam GB is a development, relief and campaigning organisation dedicated to finding lasting solutions to poverty and suffering around the world. The shops provide valuable funds to support this work.

This shop has historical significance as the very first Oxfam charity shop, established together with the first Oxfam committee that was initially called 'The Oxford Committee for Famine Relief', by Cecile Jackson-Cole (1901-1979). A blue plaque has been placed on the outside wall of the building to acknowledge this entrepreneur and philanthropist. A second plaque testifies to the year in which the shop opened: 'The first permanent Oxfam shop began trading here in December 1947.' The shop shares the street with Balliol and Trinity Colleges, in this prime location in the centre of the city.

The Broad Street shop has three floors but the ground and first floors do not seem to be selling anything of particular interest. Elaborate evening dresses fill the small amount of rail space at street level, which I presume have been donated after college balls, although it is inconceivable to me that any girl of university age would wear such mature fashions. Upstairs, there are further racks of second-hand high street label clothing for both men and women. A more unusual feature of this branch is that it is one of around fifty that is run by Oxfam as both a stamp specialist and coin collection point, accepting all used stamps, currency and other collectables, such as medals and badges.

A German edition of Wagner's Ring Cycle – *Der Ring Des Nibelungen* – on cassette tape (£44.99), sits in the window alongside a couple of cocktail dresses on mannequins as well as three volumes of *The Adventures of Sherlock Holmes* on six tapes (£7.99). Nothing here seems to give away any clues as to the fantastic music department in the basement and so I nearly miss out, not seeing the staircase leading down there until I have nearly made my exit from the shop.

Downstairs, Jill and David Partrick oversee the shop's specialist operations. In fact, books are the couple's primary interest but, having worked for many years in the specialist book section at the Henley branch, they were asked to use their experience to also manage the music collection here in Oxford. They now work between the two shops, opening up a useful line of communication. The Partricks do not own a record player themselves, which David tells me avoids any conflict of interest in the job.

Music sales make the charity a lot of money, facilitated by the expertise of its volunteer merchandisers. The Henley shop just recently sold an obscure rock record for £1000. The sleeve had been signed by the band and so David tracked down and contacted the performers, via the Internet, who asserted that the record had been given to Jimi Hendrix as a present for performing on the album,. Another example of the charity's valuable donations is the sale of a 12" LP by a folk music group from Bristol, for £1,300. The Tavistock Oxfam shop made the local news recently, having received a donation of four thousand classical records in top condition, believed to be worth £25,000. This generated a lot of publicity for the shop and it was immediately inundated with requests from interested buyers. All the shops face the problem of how to evaluate and market their stock realistically and effectively on a local level. It is the 7" vinyl records, however, that are prioritised by the connoisseurs' market and bring in the most profit. By his tone of voice David emphasises just how important these singles are to the fundraising effort.

The level of commitment demonstrated by the volunteers at Broad Street Oxfam is clearly responsible for the continued success of the shop. In a small curtained-off area at the back of the basement floor, the Partricks inspect each piece of vinyl before it goes on the shelf, consulting a stack of published music bibles and looking online to identify a record's worth after which they decide on a price for sale in the shop. There is a professional grading system of seven grades that they must follow, David explains. The price drops almost fifty per cent from one grade to the next until it becomes uneconomic to bother to sell the record. The condition of the records affects prices differently, depending on the category of music. Rock records can withstand quite a battering before buyers will reject them but classical listeners require that the vinyl is completely blemish free for sale. Each of the LPs I look at, across the various types, appears to be in immaculate condition.

Silvery CDs have been tacked to the ceiling as decoration and LPs are hung in plastic file sleeves around the walls as well as framed classic albums, all priced at £9.99. Along both sides of the length of the shop run shelves laden with collections of popular albums in both analogue and digital formats. One side is dedicated to a standard 'Rock & Pop' grouping and the other to classical music. Sheet music is offered in plastic storage boxes under the shelves along with some 78rpm records. Musical instruments are also sold as and when they are donated. Today there is a good-looking Yamaha classical guitar for sale at £45. Wagner's *Ring Cycle* as an LP box-set costs £59.

A card system is operated whereby customers are encouraged to note down their requests on call cards and the volunteer staff look out for those records as they come in. A question from another customer interrupts my conversation with the volunteers, asking if they have any German 78s from the 1940s. David confesses that he has worked in the shop for three years but has never come across any such pieces. This music outlet is as specialist as any independent record dealer, its only restriction being that it cannot dictate its stock.

ADDRESS 17 Broad Street, Oxford, OX1 3AS TELEPHONE 01865 241 333 OPEN Monday to Saturday 9:30am - 5:30pm Sunday 11am - 4pm

Customers at Oxfam, Broad Street (see page 94). Other Oxfam Music & Audio shops can be found in Exeter, Reading, Southampton, Edinburgh and Glasgow.

Tapes and CDs left outside Fircroft Trust, Surbiton (see page 90).

St Columbas's Hospice Bookshop, Morningside. ADDRESS 233 Morningside Road, Edinburgh, EH10 4QT TELEPHONE 0131 447 9008 OPEN Monday to Saturday 10am - 4pm

Punk zines at Oxfam Music, Glasgow, one of only six specialist Oxfam music shops in the UK. The Glasgow and Edinburgh shops often run charity events such as 'Oxjam', as well as other gigs and club nights, and they use MySpace to contact bands and DJs to help out on these nights. They are keen to encourage donations from people with 'proper' collections, DJ collections or promotional material as well as personal record collections. ADDRESS 171 Byres Road, Glasgow G12 8TS TELEPHONE 0141 334 7669 OPEN Monday to Saturday 10:30am - 5:30pm, Sunday 10:30am - 5pm

Boutique

Oxfam Boutique - Durham, County Durham

In the UK, Oxfam focuses on public attitudes to poverty, asylum issues, gender and race equality, and ensuring that people have sufficient income to live on.

This is a good-looking shop with traditional double frontage, located by Elvet Bridge, high up in the cobbled streets of Durham city centre. It is Oxfam's first Boutique shop and it stocks predominantly designer and desirable labels, accessories and some collectable china and glassware. The shop is painted a vibrant racing-green and the window displays have been carefully co-ordinated, absent of the usual bric-a-brac and instead sparingly ornamented with a series of quarter-scale dressmakers' dummies bound in brown string. All the goods in this shop have been taken from the other Oxfam shops around the North East to create one luxury-market brand of charity shop in a strategic location. Students form a large proportion of its customer base and in a city where fashion for a younger clientele is in great demand, many also work here as volunteers during term-time.

Inside, the shop has invested in a modish 'vintage showroom' décor, with the common features of metropolitan boutiques. A chandelier hangs at the centre of a uniform series of ridged-glass shades, beaming down warm, bright, concentrated light that is easy on the eye. A few eclectic fittings in combination with functional shop-fit display furniture work together with modern glass shelving systems to present merchandise in an attractive and

fashionable context, according to Oxfam's marketing group. Oxfam Boutique is ultimately giving the customer a familiar and comfortable experience: all the elements that have been put together to re-brand and re-present the goods on sale here are common signifiers of 'good taste', and break down any perceived division between charity and luxury retail.

Goods have been arranged in thoughtful displays on the shelves above the rails, with leather travel cases, fur stoles and jackets and framed black and white photographs collectively evoking the romance of a bygone era. All the clothing on the rails, catering to both men and women, is colour-coded and the palette looks fresh and modern. There is a specialist denim section and denim jeans are priced between £10 and £30. Prices are stencilled on traditional brown luggage tags. The Victorian counter cabinet showcases polished silverware, including both precious antiques and costume jewellery. There are sets of horn-handled cutlery in immaculate condition, in their original presentation cases. The shop also has a good glassware section with plenty of colourful, pressed-glass pieces. It offers Fairtrade food, People Tree clothing, greeting cards and a range of new jewellery.

The poster in the front window that calls for volunteers to work in the Boutique reads, 'Are you interested in fashion? Can you spot a Dior suit at twenty paces?' This exposes the uncomfortable process that charities have had to adopt in scrutinising the value of donated goods in order to sell them back to the public at a premium. Oxfam has pulled together all its resources and expertise and invested heavily in this new retail face in order to carry out this delicate operation convincingly.

ADDRESS 18 Elvet Bridge, Durham DH1 3AA TELEPHONE 0191 384 7440 OPEN Monday to Saturday 10am - 5:30pm, Sunday 11.30am - 4:30pm

Sunflower, Earl Mountbatten Hospice - Newport, Isle of Wight

The Earl Mountbatten Hospice is a non-judgmental organisation and will accept patients appropriate for palliative care, without discrimination, from all walks of life, religions and groups.

The Sunflower shop, raising money for The Earl Mountbatten Hospice, describes itself as a 'dress agency'. It is, essentially, a new breed of UK charity shop whereby the donor gets a percentage of the profit from the sale of a donated item. In this case, forty per cent goes back to the donor and sixty per cent goes to the charity shop. A sale price is agreed with the individual customer and the item is stocked for six weeks, after which time it must be collected or it is reduced in price and the total profit retained by the shop.

A consignment system encourages people to give up their more valuable commodities with the added incentive of a small personal return, as well as giving to charity. As a result, the shop is large and full of stock. It is absolutely strict in its resolve to only accept high-quality clothing, inviting donations of women's eveningwear and men's formalwear in particular. The notices posted up throughout the interior state that an item must be able to achieve a sale price of £10 in order to be accepted. Prices are on the high side, reflecting the nature of consignment. The shop used to exist on a fifty/fifty profit-share basis but VAT must be paid on the sales through a consignment system and, after the donor takes back a percentage, the shop must be left with enough money to cover its overheads as well as making a profit for its cause.

Set apart from the busy shopping centre, on one of Newport's side streets, Sunflower is fitted out in a style familiar to most high street shops. Retail manager Julie Clifton, believes that the draw of the shop is its upmarket 'boutique' feel. She remembers when the first boutique shops opened in the UK and points out that they remain a novel shopping experience, even now. She describes how the larger retail chains are destroying the possibility of a unique shopping experience. 'When everything is the same it's no wonder young people are turning to eBay to shop,' she says. Sunflower struggles to attract young customers and so Julie started up a 'retro' section. This proved unsuccessful and young people remain only a very small proportion of the clientele.

Julie tells me that she received four emails last week from charities wanting to go into the profit-share market, and seeking advice. 'Oxfam was the first to think entrepreneurially about their shops. They recognise that flea pits can't survive any more. All the nationals have followed suit and are done up beautifully. Top merchandisers have been employed by the top names in charity retailing. Topshop's Jane Shepherdson went to Oxfam. They can afford to invest in the best.' Adding a counterpoint to the positive reaction from the industry to such innovations in the sector, she forecasts a difficult

future for even the most modern variations of charity shop. She comments that, 'Everywhere you go I'd be surprised if you don't get a gloomy picture.' Last year, for the first time since the shop opened, it has shown a loss. A dress agency is hard to administer in terms of paperwork. 'The Hospice would like to get rid of it tomorrow,' she says, but like most charities, it is tied to a lease that it must see out.

There are plenty of dresses on the rails from major high street names, and some relatively upmarket boutiques, such as Jane Norman and Reiss. These garments range in price from £10 to about £60 and all price tags give an estimate of the RRP, so that the customer can judge the degree of saving. The majority of mid-range labels that pad out the stock give the impression that the historical fashion archives of our culture – the real treasures – are no longer finding their way into the charity shops. For many years I, as a charity shopper, have wondered if the rise of the vintage/second-hand clothing market has redirected the flow of goods away from third sector retail altogether, but when I put this to Julie she reassures me that this is not the case.

Plenty of valuable donations are, in fact, being made to the shop on a regular basis and customers looking for something exceptional need look no further than Julie's stockroom. Upstairs at the Lugely Street shop, which is down the road (see 'Emporium'), one small room brims with antique and designer clothing and accessories, the enduring qualities of which are instantly recognisable in their visual effect. Vintage top hats sit dust-free in their original boxes. Capes, overcoats, bags, belts, and prime examples of designer fashions from throughout the second half of the 20th century are crammed in to this small room.

Julie prefers to loan outfits from the collection in exchange for a donation (of money) to the hospice because she knows that she cannot realise the true value of such precious pieces on sale in the shops. It is more lucrative to hold on to this collection than sell it for far less than it is worth. 'I can't let things go if they're worth a lot of money,' she admits. 'I would be mortified if something slipped through.' Years of retail experience appears to have given her a strong sense of responsibility over the elusive value of charity shop merchandise. 'I don't have enough volunteers to guard the Vivienne Westwoods,' she adds.

Julie has had to identify and provide for her specific local market. Thrift is the primary concern of both the young and old alike, because they are groups with only a limited amount of disposable income. In Julie's experience, customers with more money to spend would not necessarily choose to wear Ossie Clarke. 'If you put an Ossie Clarke dress out in the shop the students will want it for two pence,' she explains. Instead Julie constructs the 'look' of the vintage realm at the Lugley Street shop, with a few select pieces and set-dressing. The retro section at the neighbouring site is aimed at people who wish to dress up in fancy dress costume. It is certainly not equipped for the serious vintage hunter.

Sunflower has recently started investing in furniture to try to increase profits. Furniture is displayed at the front of the shop and in the window. It is hoped that the recent dip in sales is merely transitional. Julie responds by saying, 'If you love clothes, you don't want to sit at the computer to buy them. The young people are eBay's main customer base and yet they're surrounded by beautiful shops. If we get it right then they will come back.'

It is inevitable that, as the technology develops, Internet shopping sites will find increasingly sophisticated ways to make online retail not simply more viable but more of an enjoyable experience. Julie does not think that the answer for charities ultimately is to invest in eBay. Charities cannot compete with the individual trader in terms of time and resources. There is also a certain expectation under a charity name, even at auction, that the pricing of goods should remain low. However, Julie feels she has no choice but to seriously consider the Internet as a way forward if she is to make a decent profit on the more valuable stock.

ADDRESS 19 Holyrood Street, Newport, Isle of Wight PO30 5AZ TELEPHONE 01983 533 933 OPEN Monday to Friday 9:30am - 4:30pm, Saturday 9:30am - 4pm

Seven Springs Boutique - Royal Tunbridge Wells, Kent

The Boutique shares its profits between Seven Springs Cheshire Home – which is part of the Leonard Cheshire Disability organisation and the largest voluntary sector provider of care and support services for disabled people – and Voluntary Action West Kent.

Seven Springs Boutique is the solo retail venture of two charities. Set up initially to raise money for Seven Springs Cheshire Home, the shop now shares its profits with a partner charity, Voluntary Action West Kent. Leonard Cheshire, who married Sue Ryder, founded the disabled charity Leonard Cheshire Disability in 1948 and the charity shop in 1972, making it the oldest in Tunbridge Wells.

More than thirty years before charity shops began to rebrand themselves, Seven Springs Boutique took the decision to obscure its charity status and present itself as a high quality ladies' fashion outlet. It sells no menswear or children's clothing and its bijou scale suits its 'boutique' nomination. Only recently has the shop taken on bric-a-brac, which now comprises a significant proportion of the sales and also generates interest amongst the groups not catered for in the clothing section. Men come in, for the most part, to look at the CDs and records and there is a selection of toys and games to occupy the children.

Initially there was a strong resistance from staff to taking in so much bric-a-brac but public demand forced the change of policy. 'We have to listen to what people want and move with the times,' says voluntary manager Dorothy Selvey. 'The positive outcome of the wide range of goods the shop now stocks is that, due to our size, we have to be highly selective about what we sell.'

The high street seasonal sales in turn affect the charity shop's profits and Seven Springs holds a sale itself to redress the balance. The second week of its sale sees prices slashed to £1, but occasionally the shop is left with some decent goods. If a good quality garment has not sold for this negligible amount then it must be ruthlessly disposed of. Any clothes that do not sell or are not fit for sale are sold on, by weight, to a firm called Gemini, which further sorts the goods for charitable distribution and reuse abroad or for recycling. This is a recent development from a previous arrangement with the Seven Springs Home who took rag-bags for its jumble sale. When the Home stopped hosting the annual sale the charity shop had to find alternative avenues for the disposal of leftover clothing.

The clothes that are kept for sale are sorted and priced by the volunteers, reflecting their elderly tastes. There is an iron and ironing-board visible through the open doorway into the back room and all the clothes are ordered by size. Dorothy points out to me the uniform black clothes hangers, as an example of the level of detail considered in maintaining an orderly presentation of the merchandise. The front window is a neat and attractive display of china, jewellery, glassware and earthenware, spread across a carpeted 'stage' that is screened off from the shop by a modest net curtain.

Seven Springs Boutique is located off the beaten track and away from the town centre in Tunbridge Wells, and relies on its immediate local and loyal band of customers rather than passers-by. It is run entirely by volunteers, many of whom have worked here for several years. The majority are elderly women and parishioners of St. Augustine's Catholic Church across the road. For many years the women have taken turns to look after the shop single-handedly, but Dorothy now insists that they work in pairs for safety. This puts a strain on manpower, however, and despite its Volunteer Service associate the Boutique is currently experiencing a volunteer crisis. It is frequently forced to close due to a lack of staff.

The shop has lost several of its dedicated volunteers over the past year. If it is to survive its elderly workforce it needs to recruit new people. A local language school student recently joined the team but the quiet location of the shop could not fulfill her needs. Dorothy has run adverts in local newspapers, churches, shops, libraries and the local ladies' golf club but she has not yet had a positive response. She is conscious of the earnest tone in citing the rewarding or worthwhile benefits to volunteer work, recognising the need to promote incentives beyond that of 'doing good' and to point out other, self-interested advantages to working in a charity shop. On an informal basis, volunteers who may be keen on fashion or antiques have first-pickings on the purchase of donations that come in and Dorothy considers advertising this motivation to a younger group.

ADDRESS 14 Crescent Road, Tunbridge Wells, Kent TN1 2LU TELEPHONE 01892 522 002 OPEN Monday to Friday (except Wednesday - closed) 10am - 4pm, Saturday 10am - 1pm

Oxfam Sustainable Fashion Boutique - Chelsea, London

Oxfam supports schools and communities worldwide and campaigns for funds and better policies from governments on education.

For a long time Oxfam has been synonymous in the UK with second-hand clothing and its ubiquitous charity shops have been a humble mainstay of the country's high streets. In more recent years, it became the first to develop the old charity retail model into increasingly sophisticated variations on specialist themes, the most recent of which is its Sustainable Fashion Boutique.

This Chelsea branch is one of three Sustainable Fashion Boutiques that opened in London in May 2008, all specialising in vintage, second-hand, re-styled and customised fashion in both womenswear and menswear ranges. The concept is a further development in the unique Durham Boutique shop in that donated stock has been mobilised, rebranded and re-appropriated over four speciality clothing ranges that explore themes of provenance and recycling in fashion. The other Sustainable Boutiques are located in Portobello and Chiswick and the charity aims to open a national network of up to twenty-five such shops in other upmarket urban areas across the country within the next two years, with the ambition of setting a new benchmark for sustainable fashion in the luxury marketplace.

Oxfam has a rich history in experimentation with fashion branding, having employed in its service some of the most respected names in the industry to turn around the perceived charity shop stereotype that its executives believe limits its customer base. The Boutiques have been produced with the help of creative consultant Jane Shepherdson, former fashion director at Topshop, widely credited with reversing the chain's fortunes during her time as brand director. Since a high water mark at the turn of the century, Oxfam shops' profits have slumped, due to pressures affecting the entire non-profit sector, and the charity has invested heavily in this project to boost sales with a new audience and renewed interest, supported by a different clothing business model. The average Oxfam sale is around £20, increasing thirty per cent across the three Boutiques since they opened and reaping dividends for the company overall by helping to make Oxfam Britain's most lucrative charity shop chain, with profits of £21 million.

To mark the launch, Shepherdson and the Oxfam team pulled in the support of some of Britain's most influential young designers to produce one-off pieces from donated clothing and fabrics, ranging from evening gowns to duvet covers. The seven reworked pieces, from Giles Deacon, Henry Holland, Christopher Kane, Jonathan Saunders, Richard Sorger, Jens Laugesen and Stephen Jones, were unveiled at the Westbourne Grove shop launch, displayed in the window, in advance of their sale at auction on eBay, to raise money for the charity. Oxfam have collected donations by distributing 'givvy' bags at London Fashion Week and branded black and white tuk-tuks have circulated

the Boutique vicinities to gather contributions.

This shop, just off Chelsea's main high street, has been transformed from an Oxfam Originals shop and fits very well with the Kings Road's history as a pioneering boutique destination and symbol of counter-culture since the 1960s. Of course, gentrification of the area followed and it is now one of the most high end fashion-shopping destinations in London. Chelsea Oxfam has always enjoyed above average value donations, due to its privileged location. Like its other Boutique stores, its local clientele and regular stream of tourist shoppers appear to have a taste for, as well as the means to afford, the top designer labels.

The range of donated garments on offer in the shop has been branded 'Loved for Longer' and has been pre-sorted to include only the best garments, to make it easier for shoppers to find items of interest. Retail head, Sarah Farquhar, says, 'Women don't have time to spend hours looking for that special piece. We've just done the rummaging for them.' The label declares, 'This item was cherished by someone else.' It makes an appeal to the purchaser; 'If you ever tire of this item simply take it to your local Oxfam and we'll sell it to someone else.' Oxfam wants to see an increase in people who will 'shop and drop' under one roof in its Boutiques.

'Reinvented' is a collection of pieces donated to Oxfam and reworked by young UK designers including Defraye, Junk (Jumble) and London College of Fashion students. Offering them an opportunity to test their products commercially, the students are paid fifty per cent of the retail price, to encourage them to churn out a regular supply. The Reinvented label says, 'This item was something else when it was donated to Oxfam.' All the refashioned and embellished garments are one of a kind with a good quality finish, which therefore command a higher price than the usual Oxfam clothes. One patchwork dress, made up of five vintage donations, costs £110. 'Made with Love' is a selection of accessories produced by volunteers, again reworking donated pieces.

'Good Fashion Sense' is a series of clothes and accessories that are organic, recycled, made from alternative fibres or by labels working towards Fair Trade accreditation. Manufacturers include Junky Styling, Sea Salt and Amana. The Fairtrade Foundation or IFAT fashion and accessories labels People Tree, Green Knickers, Casa Copenhagen and Wright and Teague aim to connect consumers with producers who tend to work on a small scale and engage traditional skills. They claim to be 'environmentally friendly' products, made by companies with the support of micro credit schemes to help with training, marketing and business development, and enabling people to achieve a fair wage.

The backdrop for the clothes echoes the high-end bohemian shopping environments of the Kings Road. The furniture has been donated by a local interiors company – wrought iron rail units with glass shelving organize the clothes in this small space – and reclaimed hospital flooring looks good under low-energy lighting. Many of the hangers are unique, handmade and padded with satin fabrics and bows. A pair of open-toed Prada sandals (£80) sit demurely on antique wooden shelves beside vintage handbags (£35) and jewellery by Wright and Teague. Antique lace collars (£18) adorn the mannequins.

Oxfam Chief Executive Barbara Stocking says that the charity is responding to customers' requests for 'a contemporary shopping experience'. Sarah Farquhar adds, 'Shoppers in many towns and cities are very sophisticated and they want to see better retail standards from charity shops than just a pile of old books.' The Boutiques have been criticised for being 'elitist' and for taking away the thrill of the chase, in an ordinary Oxfam store, and the sweat out of a rummage, but Farquhar thinks that this view is outdated. She insists that the Boutiques are about inclusivity, expressing her hope that the new look and others like it will entice a whole new breed of Oxfam shopper, with more customers who choose to shop in Oxfam rather than who need to.

ADDRESS 123a Shawfield Street, London SW3 4PL TELEPHONE 020 7351 7979 OPEN Monday to Saturday 10am - 6pm

Scarlet, St. Clare Hospice - Buckhurst Hill, Essex

The St. Clare Hospice shops exist solely to raise money for and awareness of St. Clare Hospice.

This is a ladies' boutique selling predominantly designer clothing. It is located along the small, intimate high street of a cosy, suburban neighbourhood. Money has been spent on a lighting scheme that creates the right mood for an upmarket establishment, replacing the usual foam-tiled, strip-light ceiling familiar to businesses that place less emphasis on appearance or lack the resources to test the benefits of modernisation. The shop has both the feel of directed company branding – with its retail industry standard shop fascia and fit-out – and local autonomy – selling local donations and reflecting very obviously the tastes and allegiances of residents who both buy and donate the goods.

The retail unit is narrow and deep, its size exaggerated by the effect of plenty of mirrors and by the hardwood strip flooring that runs from the front

to the back of the shop. Chrome rails and glass shelving line the walls, broken up by a few glass cabinets that display goods under lock and key. As well as donated goods, Scarlet sells a lot of bought-in goods that are placed around the top shelves, above the rails of clothes, and seem to influence the overall style of all merchandise. These include printed gift boxes, hat-boxes, vanity cases, curious ornaments and mantelpiece objects, all covered in unifying floral prints and gestural painted lifestyle imagery.

All the clothes on the rails have been steamed beautifully and grouped by colour so that tops and jackets are mixed together with trousers and skirts. There appears to be a lot of pastel shades, 'for the spring,' I am told. There is a good quantity of designer brand jeans at around £20 a pair. Other labels that crop up throughout the rails are Gerry Weber, Jaeger, Jigsaw and Whistles, selling for up to £30. There is nothing that is not absolutely contemporary and no more than a couple of seasons behind from their brand shops. There are no unconventional pieces or vintage garments and nothing is old enough to look at all scruffy or particularly worn. I get the impression that no item here has been through the wash more than a few times and so, for the most part, these clothes are mainstream high street fashion, selling at about half the price. There is a small menswear section too. The changing room is a swathe of cream curtains around a generously proportioned chrome rail, in the back of the shop.

The only hint that this is a charity shop is the pin-board by the front door which is covered in printed leaflets promoting the charity and its current works and news. This is the only specialist shop run by St. Clare and it has clearly invested a lot in the enterprise. When I start asking questions about the shop the manager asks me suspiciously if I work for another charity. 'We have to be careful in case other shops spy on us and copy our ideas. Competition would kill us,' she explains.

The shop fills up suddenly whilst I am there and I can see that the customers are familiar with and therefore comfortable in this type of shopping environment. The manager and her assistant standing at the counter are very similar in appearance to their clientele. They understand their customers and tailor the shop to suit their common needs, offering a boutique shopping experience for the older, financially stable lady. There are labels of interest to all tastes here, if not always the most desirable examples of those brands.

ADDRESS 46 Queens Road, Buckhurst Hill, Essex 1G9 5BY TELEPHONE 020 8505 5110 OPEN Monday to Saturday 9:15 am - 5:15pm

The Geranium Shop, Greater London Fund For The Blind - Marylebone, London

The GLFB was established to unify the collection of funds on behalf of several blind welfare charities, enabling them to focus their attention on the prime task of helping to improve the lives of visually impaired people in London.

The Greater London Fund for the Blind runs eighteen charity shops across the capital, called Geranium shops. The charity has operated a shop in the central Marylebone area of London for over twenty years, although it has been at its current address for just over eight years, having had to move due to high rent at its previous location. It is now situated just off the high street but retains a strong presence in the area of the commercial thoroughfare, aided by its close proximity to another charity shop, and together they create a diverse attraction. The Marylebone shop does not brand itself any differently to the other Geranium branches and yet its bijou scale and choice stock lifts its shabby décor into that of an old-fashioned junkshop boutique setting. This, in turn, attracts a suitable calibre of donation, notably better than that of its charity neighbour, Barnardo's.

The charity's Retail Manager, Lorraine Foot, ran three shops of her own before coming to work for the Geranium trading company. She visits the shops in rotation every three months for assessment but otherwise the individual businesses are self-sufficient. Marylebone, she tells me, is still a 'carrier bag' shop, and manages to stock itself entirely with doorstep donations rather than depending on the provision of a pre-sorted stock, collected from its other shops. There is a professional and forward-thinking approach to the daily running of the shop. The volunteer manager leads regular two-week inductions and training for new volunteers. The government also offers optional funded courses that lead to qualifications in Customer Service and Shop Management, which teach well-established retail marketing strategies such as colour coding and pricing psychology.

This shop chooses not to coordinate its stock by colour as the manager believes that with a mixed selection the customer might find something unexpected. Lorraine provides all shops with a pricing guide, which suggests that a blouse is valued at between £3 and £5, and a ladies' suit is around £30. I come across a mustard yellow 70s vintage YSL two-piece for £60, as an example of the premium mark-up on that scale. The sizing in womenswear tends to be small, reflecting the typically svelte physique of local residents, and the styling is mature, yet classic. There are a few contemporary top-name brands as well as the usual high street names but many of the clothes sport obscure boutique labels.

The bric-a-brac and homeware collections are as much of a lure as the shop's clothing. A hand-painted 1930s bone china tea set is offered for £22. Silver-plated picture frames, brooches, paperweights, larger vases and crafted glass pieces are affordable to a wider public than their original price-tags courted. The main window display faces inwards into the shop. A brown, carpeted platform displays a pair of ornate brass wall-mounted lights, mirrors, decorative vases and a small side table, ornamented with African and oriental crafts, altogether reminiscent of the colonial fashions of the 20th century. In front, a smaller collection of knick-knacks includes pots, dishes and toiletries dispensers as well as a more practical miscellany, such as a handsaw, a selection of spectacles cases and a full set of 70s Habitat coffee cups.

The walls are painted a pea green and the clothes hangers are coordinated in bright green plastic. Framed pictures hang on the walls. Around the room, shelves are full of VHS tapes, a few books, records, CDs and cassette tapes. Board games perch on top and mens' clothing hangs beneath. Womenswear takes up a central dress rail and the opposite wall. A vast collection of accessories softens the room with patterned textiles. Bags and hats hang from every opportune protrusion and there is a concentrated collection of ties, headscarves, belts and necklaces on hooks fixed to wooden-slatted storage cupboard doors by the desk. A glass presentation case for jewellery is next to the till and displays perfume bottles, sunglasses, make-up compacts, ornamental boxes and bottles for the dressing table, as well as the silver and costume jewellery stocks, collectively illuminated by the warm light of a table lamp. Old theatre programmes and opera glasses add an element of theatricality.

ADDRESS 4 George Street, Marylebone, London W1U 3QU TELEPHONE 020 7935 1790 OPEN Monday to Saturday 10am - 5pm

British Red Cross Boutique - Swiss Cottage, London

The BRC is a volunteer-led humanitarian organisation that helps people in crisis, in the United Kingdom and overseas.

This is one of the first BRC shops to have been revamped, as part of a new re-branding scheme, set off by its lucrative and renowned flagship shop in Chelsea. It occupies the corner of an elegant Arts and Crafts building with original stained-glass windowpanes, on the anonymous thoroughfare that is the Finchley Road. The area has been a popular destination for charity shoppers for many years due to a small concentration of good charity shops along the main road (see 'Antiques and Collectables') and on West End Lane. A 'boutique' denomination shows the charity shop's ambitions to appeal to this affluent catchment. The Chelsea shop does not grant itself this status, despite having far more salubrious stock, but the nature of the area and the position of commerce within it means that the Swiss Cottage shop must quickly establish a reputation for being out of the ordinary and better than average.

Garments on the rails are colourful, highly-patterned and collectively make BRC Boutique immediately recognisable as a predominantly 'retro' fashion shop, geared towards a younger clientele. There are rails of carefully edited retro and vintage items as well as the more fun fancy-dress pieces. Flicking through the clothes I find that they are peppered with many contemporary designer labels, and the prices are reasonable. A brand new pair of leopard-print APC jeans is £15. A Vivienne Westwood cardigan is £35, in good condition. There are also plenty of fashionable shoes, bags and belts, loosely accessorising items throughout the shop. Belts range in price from £1.50 to £12 and shoes are priced at between £10 and £25. 'Bags of Style' is the tag line on one of several marketing posters, cutouts and leaflets around the shelves, styling the products with an emphasis on top-line over retrograde qualities.

BRC Boutique has the feel of a fancy dressing-up box, accented by theatrical fur stoles and sparkle. A decent menswear section dominates one corner of the shop and errs on the more practical side of dressing for occasion. The single changing room with no mirror is basically just a very small patch of standing room shielded by a curtain. The prospect puts me off trying and buying any of the clothes I have picked up: a 1970s YSL Rive Gauche blue linen jacket for £32, a pure wool hand-embroidered kaftan for £12.50 and the APC jeans. The wood-panelled walls and paintwork are the muted colours of English Heritage. The clothes stand out on the simple portable rails and upscale, uniform wooden hangers. Every item has been colour coordinated as well as labelled by size. Only the workaday notice board by the till and closer inspection of the flyers and leaflets revealing publicity on a charitable theme give away the fact that this establishment is a charity shop.

I ask the sole assistant managing the shop whether their methods for pre-sorting clothes are time-consuming. She tells me that the items come ready-priced from the warehouse and they are selected especially to support the theme of the shop. Rather than supplement stock donated directly to the shop it is altogether traded in-house with more suitable collections. The liberated stock is then distributed around the regular BRC shops, shredded for recycling or exported for reuse in deprived areas aided by the charity. There is a delivery and pick-up at the Boutique four times a week. In contrast to retail's standard 'odd prices' and the perception of value, the price endings here are even numbers, in line with high-end business that has begun to readily differentiate itself by a noticeable 'open' pricing system. The psychology applied to the marketing of this shop is sophisticated even if it is transparent. In the end, the Boutique customers must be reminded of the purpose behind the operation. Discouraging customers from asking for a discount on items, a sign by the till delivers a jaded request, 'Please do not ask for a reduction. This is a charity shop.'

ADDRESS 307 Finchley Road, London NW3 6EH TELEPHONE 020 7435 9828 OPEN Monday to Saturday 10am - 5pm

All Dressed Up, Lindsey Lodge, Scunthorpe is a boutique-style shop with dress agency facilities for regular clients. Gift vouchers are available. ADDRESS 8 Ravendale Street (North), Scunthorpe, North Lincolnshire, DN15 6NE TELEPHONE 01724 854 219 OPEN Monday to Saturday 9:30am - 4pm

'Turn your Prada into £ and your Couture into Cash and Care,' at Because, Butterwick. ADDRESS 9 Market Row, Barkers Arcade, Northallerton, North Yorkshire DL7 8LN TELEPHONE 01609 773 737 OPEN Monday to Saturday 10am - 5pm (closed one lunchtime)

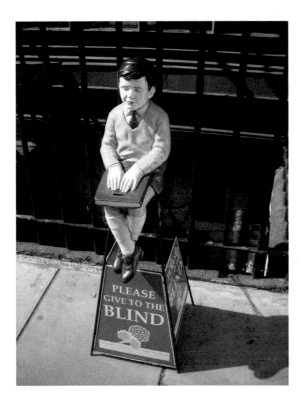

Tea set and collection box at Geranium Shop, Marylebone (see page 112)

An inspiring interior at Shelter, Newcastle. ADDDRESS 20, Nun Street, Newcastle Upon Tyne, Tyne and Wear NE1 5AQ TELEPHONE 0191 230 3910 OPEN Monday to Saturday 9am - 5pm

Previously a Wishes branch of Cancer Research, Cancer Research Pinner has recently had a make-over, transforming it into an up-market boutique-style shop. ADDDRESS 26, Bridge St, Pinner, Middlesex HA5 3HR TELEPHONE 020 8866 4989 OPEN Monday to Saturday 9am - 5:30pm

Stylishly presented goods on sale at Martlets, Lewes. ADDRESS 53 High Street, Lewes
BN7 1XE TELEPHONE 01273 478 560 OPEN Monday to Saturday 10am - 4.30pm

BRIDAL

St. Catherine's Hospice - Preston, Lancashire

Fundraising on behalf of St. Catherine's Hospice, the charity shops provides a focal point for many supporters, or for those who have become personally involved with the Hospice.

Located in a prime spot at the back of the bus station and the St. John's Shopping Centre, facing the vast Victorian structure of the covered Market Square, is the St. Catherine's Hospice Shop, specialising in bridalwear. The second floor of this relatively grand-scale shop houses an outstanding wedding department. Packed with dresses of all varieties, it also manages to squeeze some bridesmaid's dresses on to a few rails and some carefully selected 'mother of the bride' outfits. There is a good range of gentlemen's garb too, such as tailcoats for the groom and best man as well as a few pageboy outfits.

On the ground floor there are plenty more dresses, the majority of them evening or occasionwear and tiaras, hair-accessories and jewellery spill out of the till-counter cabinet. Quality undergarments and accessories are distributed here and there throughout the shop. Shoes sit neatly in pairs around the edge of the floor like the new blooms in brightly coloured flowerbeds. The many rails are so stuffed with clothes they appear to be climbing the walls and the high ceiling gives the stock a dramatic backdrop. The customer is naturally drawn towards the tall staircase at the back of the shop, where hats and headpieces are displayed along the ascending wall. Upstairs mothers and daughters browse the rails of dresses together. 'There is always someone on hand to help them look for the right dress at the right price and all the extras that come after that,' says one of the two elderly volunteers. The shop also runs a hire service, on selected items.

Rather than competing with the other bridal shops in Preston, of which there are several, St. Catherine's operates with their help. Dan Kerr, further along Lancaster Road, gets in new stock at the end of every year and donates the old stock, in brand new condition, to the Hospice. St. Catherine's has operated a shop on these premises for eight years and it has gained a reputation not just with local customers but amongst the other local shops as well. Businesses that close down often give the last of their stock to the shop, which recently received seventy sample dresses as a donation. This stock is combined with a majority of second-hand bridalwear, skimmed from the other Hospice shops outside of Preston, which is donated by local individuals. I ask if it took people time to accept buying second-hand clothes for such an all-important occasion. Manager, Cath, tells me that the shop started up with only second-hand dresses and that it has never had a problem selling them. The shop was as successful then as it is today.

Many of the dresses here still have their original price tags on them so the bride can see how much she is saving. Ninety per cent of the stock now is new, donated. 'They have the dress they want but they know the money has gone to a good cause and they have been thrifty in buying it. They feel very good about buying here,' says Cath. Some of the dresses have original price tags of around £1000 but the most the shop has ever charged for a dress, Cath tells me, is £350, for a quite exceptional garment. A hand-written sign in the window advertises prices starting at £30, and there are quite a few dresses available at that modest level. On average though, the prices range between £100 and £150.

'Customers, brides-to-be, tend to come in the shop several times to gather everything they need before the wedding. First they come in to look and then they come back with their bridesmaids. Because a wedding is often a long-planned event, people end up spending quite a lot of money here, but they know that they are saving a lot too. Some of the girls are on a shoestring budget and we are happy to be able to help them,' adds Cath. The incentive to spend comes with the knowledge that the money will go to charity. Not only that but it is fundraising for a local hospice. 'Local customers always know someone who knows someone who's been cared for by the Hospice. Many of the girls' parents or grandparents have died in the Hospice and they want to buy from or donate to the Hospice because it means something to them.' For many local people buying a wedding dress here takes on a profound meaning.

ADDRESS St. Catherine's Hospice, 55–56A Lancaster Road, Preston PR1 1DD
TELEPHONE 01772 884 470 OPEN Monday to Saturday, 10am - 4pm.

St. Ann's Hospice - Cheadle, Greater Manchester

St Ann's Hospice aims to improve the quality of life of people living with life-threatening illnesses in Greater Manchester, whilst supporting their families and carers.

This is perhaps the most interesting and unusual of the shop interiors I have come across. Inhabiting the old Wienholt bakery and tearooms, St. Ann's has an original Art Deco interior, preserved in immaculate condition and complete with café signage throughout. The charity took over the building to sell its donated goods and maintained the upstairs tearooms, but it could not make enough money to cover overheads. It has subsequently dedicated the upstairs salon, in all its appropriate splendour, to bridalwear.

Gold tiles cover the mid section of the walls and the Deco designs in the woodwork are painted pale pink and mint green. Against this period backdrop, romantically styled wedding dresses hang on rails in a carpeted room of grand proportions that overlooks the street. For sale are 'pre-loved' and new dresses, shoes, tiaras and bridesmaid outfits. There are also a few items for the groom and pageboy. A large changing room has been created by hanging a series of curtains that partition one corner of the salon, making a relaxed viewing area with gentle lighting and soft furnishings, 'perfect for those all important wedding advisors,' says St Ann's manager, Christine Hampton.

'It is a well known fact that weddings cost a fortune these days and if a bride wants to look her best this often means spending an equally hefty sum on a dress,' Christine continues. Here, brand new end-of-line dresses that have been donated by local bridal shops start at just £50 and the average dress ranges between £80 and £200. The shop also runs a bridal fair for two weeks every year providing a 'one-stop shop' for bridalwear, headdresses, shoes and bridesmaid dresses. In March, it replenishes the stock with a whole new line of dresses.

'The quality of the bridalwear we receive is incredible. Many of the dresses that are given to us still have the original price tag on,' explains Christine. 'We had one lady in last week who had heard about the dresses that we had in

stock and looked us up on the Internet. Word is obviously starting to spread that an affordable dress for that special day really does exist!'

I work my way around the bridal salon and out on to the landing where there is a fine selection of vintage and modern hats, accompanied by an elaborate display of flowers in a tall vase on a plinth. The original 'tearoom' sign points straight ahead, to a back room now occupied by the charity's sorting office. Built in to the corner at the bottom of the stairs is a beautiful chrome and glass display cabinet that showcases wedding paraphernalia. To the customers downstairs, this is the only indication of the treasures above. In fact, from the outside, the geometric stained-glass panels in the top of the front windows are the only sign that this building might house an unusual collection. On first impression this is a traditional charity shop selling the standard range of donated goods.

The ground floor shop sells second-hand clothing for both women and men. There is a notably large collection of children's clothes and a small amount of bric-a-brac. The till counter cabinet brims with tiaras and further accessories for the hair and head, as well as some of the more precious accessory pieces to compliment the bridalwear.

This charity shop's exceptional charm lies in its unobtrusive presence within an elegant setting that seems to resonate with the 'old-fashioned' principles of shop-keeping. Along the high street there are the usual charity shop suspects, all refitted with modern shop design interiors. The dying embers of a more diverse and culturally vibrant high street are evident - the old Wool Shop has long gone but W. Hulme 'Farm Produce' is still trading.

ADDRESS 3 High Street, Cheadle, Cheshire SK8 1AX TELEPHONE 0161 428 5949 OPEN Monday to Saturday 9:30am - 4:30pm

CLIC Sargent, Exmouth, Devon

The CLIC Sargent Research Unit within the Department of Cellular and Molecular Medicine, at the University of Bristol, was set up in 1985 to study the fundamental changes that cause cancers to develop in children.

All the stock in this small, dedicated bridal shop is brand new, acquired by the charity's head office in Bristol and distributed to this Exmouth branch. There are around one hundred and twenty dresses currently in stock, provided in two deliveries since the shop opened last May. The charity's main shop on The Strand previously housed a Bridal Suite upstairs, stocking both new and old wedding dresses, but sales were slow and the shop found it difficult to distinguish the valuable new collections from the worn garments and to establish itself as an up-market bridal specialist, despite readily advertising its 'new gowns'.

Deputy manager Hayley Richardson believes brides were reluctant to buy a dress in this context because the second-hand stigma was off-putting on such an emotional occasion where superstition may be rife. When the shop unit on Albion Street became available, the charity seized the opportunity to move its new stock. The landlord helped it to launch its new venture by providing the space for the first six months rent-free.

The Strand branch continues to stock second-hand wedding dresses, which it sells to those customers who are financially restricted and often to students looking for fancy dress costumes. There is currently a large collection of around fifty unique, hand-made bridesmaid dresses, connected by a fairytale themed thread, all donated by one local seamstress who recently closed her business.

Albion Street is a semi-residential area that creates an intimate setting for the bridal boutique. All the dresses in the front room of the shop, visible on two sides to the street, are the more elaborate designs and the traditional 'meringue' dresses, with crinolines. This collection is confined to ivory tones, which contributes to a sleek and unified appearance. Through an arched open doorway and a step down in to the back room of the shop there is a changing room, along with a further collection of white dresses with pared-down, A-line designs.

The collection comprises contemporary, end-of-line and unique, commissioned dresses. There are many one-off pieces by named designers, such as Ronald Joyce and Augusta Jones. Prices are dictated by head office and the most expensive dress here is around £500, in contrast with the 'sale rail' dresses, priced between £50 and £100. Hayley believes these represent savings of as much as seventy-five per cent of the original price.

New tiaras cost £24.99. 'Prom' time brings with it a boost in the sale of accessories. There are plenty of accessories for both bride and groom, although the groom is not catered for in clothing. The shop tried stocking second-hand tailcoats but the collection did not take off and the charity felt that worn clothing would taint the image of the shop's new stock. CLIC Sargent now sells its dresses consistently throughout the year, with sales only noticeably affected by wet weather. The shop can sell as many as three dresses in a week and, rather than being absorbed into the charity's general reserve, the proceeds from this particular shop help to fund the two CLIC Sargent nurses based at the Royal Devon and Exeter Hospital in Exeter.

ADDRESS 19a Albion Street, Exmouth, Devon, EX8 TELEPHONE 01395 225 055 OPEN Tuesday to Saturday 10am - 4pm

St. Luke's Hospice Shop - Northwich, Cheshire

St Luke's Hospice is a small hospice situated in Winsford that cares for people living in the mid and south Cheshire area.

This two-storey shop in the small Cheshire town of Northwich has a wide variety of goods on sale, but its specialties are art and, more predominantly, wedding attire. Framed prints and original artworks on canvas cover the two walls of the stairwell and landing, leading to the upstairs open-plan room that is devoted to wedding dresses and accessories for the bride, bridesmaids and mother of the bride. This enterprise is still in its early stages, yet in less than twelve months the shop has developed a fully comprehensive bridal department, advertising itself also to carnival and prom queens.

There used to be another, mainstream bridal shop in Northwich, directly opposite St. Luke's on the main pedestrian street, but this closed down some time ago. When both shops operated together no channel of communication between operations was opened up but St. Luke's manager, Susie Derbyshire, does not feel that they were in competition with each other. She believes that the customer has already made their decision before they come in to the shop to buy second-hand. St. Luke's still makes most of its profits on donated womenswear but it sells a wedding dress on average once every couple of weeks throughout the year, making it a successful business that supports all other sales and increases profit per unit.

Susie is reluctant to suggest why a bride-to-be might choose to buy from the Hospice or how she might feel about buying second-hand for her all-important wedding day; she believes the incentive to be a very personal one. She speculates on a series of very practical motivations such as a lack of money or a personal relationship to the Hospice itself by way of a relative who has received care there. She suggests that as many as fifty per cent of customers come in to the shop because they are aware, to varying degrees, of the service that the Hospice provides and its fundraising needs. Customers serve the interests of their community when they shop here and their investment in a local healthcare service may be of benefit to themselves also.

The group of customers that are less interested in the specific purpose of the shop may simply choose to shop at St. Luke's on a more general principle of charity, Susie suggests. Many are simply looking for thrift opportunity and she is aware that charity shopping has become a common pastime, woven into the historic concerns of shopping and provisioning. 'If they can find a next-to-new Marks and Spencer top on our rails for cheaper then why would they go to Marks and Spencer?' she asks, rhetorically. The incentive to go shopping and to do 'good', is an added bonus.

Susie is proactive in keeping the shop looking clean, tidy and interesting. She gathered fourteen years of experience as a volunteer for a national chain of charity shops before taking on the role of assistant manager and then manager here at St. Luke's. 'Unless employees are prepared to go the extra mile, she says, the shops remain dull and don't make the kind of money needed by the charity. They must usually commit to a lease and if profits aren't coming in then the shops become a burden rather than a vital part of the business.' Job satisfaction also plays a major role for Susie and the volunteers, who host fashion shows and theme window displays on a weekly basis to keep themselves busy and interested as well as their customers. It takes at least two hours to change the window and, because of the location of the entrance door, this must be conducted when the shop is closed.

Although the shop has no regular retail benefactor of new bridalwear it regularly receives brand new dresses, often from women who have planned a wedding that has not ultimately come about. This scenario apparently explains the many dresses on the rails that have retained their original price tags. The pricing policy applied by the staff here is to imagine the original retail value and then establish a new price that is approximately less than half. The range of prices on the rails is between £30 and £240.

St. Luke's is restricted to fundraising only within a designated local area, according to its catchment that is agreed by the local authority and other regional hospices. It can therefore be free to advise and support other neighbouring hospice shops without a conflict of interests. The geographic boundary also serves St. Luke's, by way of its own internal network. The close proximity of the St Luke's branches means that they can easily exchange and rotate stock, out of which specialisms have developed. In turn, customers can travel easily between the shops for the specialist items they require.

The Middlewich shop has a particularly good range of childrenswear and toys, doing well because the town is small and does not have a children's clothes shop. It also has a book section and regularly hosts signed book sales although, like most charity shops, it stockpiles its most valuable books for auction. The St. Luke's shops all rotate their stock up to three times a week and distribute a notably good range of popular-name brands of pottery like Wedgwood, Spode and Royal Doulton, as well as gifts and kitchenware (see 'Furniture').

ADDRESS 99a Witton Street, Northwich, Cheshire CW9 5AB TELEPHONE 01606 490 56 OPEN Monday to Saturday 9:30am - 4:30pm

Camden Brides, Hospice in the Weald - Tunbridge Wells, Kent

The Hospice has an education department that plays an important part in providing training and staff development to professionals working both in Palliative care and in other generic settings.

This charity shop occupies a large detached corner building that incorporates two identical ground floor shop units, married visually by consistent paintwork in green and white. Tunbridge Wells is a Georgian 'middle England' spa town that lies across the Kent boundary with East Sussex, on the northern edge of the Weald countryside, and derives a large portion of its income from tourism. Of the charity's eleven Hospice shops that all benefit from the general level of wealth the across the region, this specialist shop is situated in an area of the town that is deemed of relatively low-status.

There are few signs from the front of the shop that it has any specialism at all. A staple example of the traditional meringue wedding dress dwells within the flower-embellished frame of the main front window and the passer-by might easily fail to notice further evidence in one of the bay windows above, that is stencilled 'Camden Brides' across the glass. Even the dressed mannequins that look out of the two first floor windows do not convey the extent of stock available in the upstairs warren of rooms that supplement the apparently small ground floor shop and offer a full selection of carefully categorised clothing.

I have chosen to include this profile in the Bridal section of the book because the 'bridalwear showroom', Camden Brides, is the focus for the shop's modest self-promotion. In addition to its bridal stock on the first floor, staff have put together a 'retro' room, as well as a room devoted to women's eveningwear and occasionwear and another to men's formalwear. In fact, the shop manager, Iain Stocker, reveals to me that the retro department has proven to be the shop's true success, providing more frequent and consistent sales than any other collection of goods. The shop might sell one wedding dress every couple of weeks and, at various stages in their planning, prospective brides visit the shop throughout the year. Sales of accessories are far more frequent, not only for weddings but for hen nights and fancy dress parties.

For the time being the shop depends on word-of-mouth to advertise itself as a unique fashion resource. Customers are advised to make an appointment to access the upstairs showrooms. Steep stairs are a health and safety issue and there isn't always sufficient staff to monitor or help customers, away from the main shop floor. Advertising costs money and the question of justifying such an expense forces the management to be tentative.

Struggling to bring money to the area, Camden Road businesses and the local authority have got together to create a website to help raise its profile as an enticing shopping street, boldly asking 'Have you discovered us yet?' A charity shop in this part of town clearly cannot demand the highest prices. Hospice in the Weald recently received a huge donation of brand new Maxmara clothes, keeping the shop in good stock for months to come. A pair of trousers that would sell for well over £100, new in the Maxmara shop, is priced here at £6.

A lot of the pricing is set from above at Hospice in the Weald. Retail co-ordinators from the head office visit the shop regularly to check pricing and occasionally extract the more valuable pieces to sell on eBay on behalf of the

charity. Iain uses the Internet and sites such as eBay himself to cross-reference stock with its common value, which he then undercuts fractionally for sale in the shop. Aware that he must give up a degree of the potential profit on an item for the sake of his customers, Iain comments, 'We need each other. Of course, I have to make sure we're not selling something for £3 if it's worth £300 but otherwise we accept a certain compromise.'

Camden Brides is well-stocked with traditional wedding dresses and complimentary fairytale bridesmaid dresses that reflect the colour spectrum of garden hydrangea. In a subsidiary bridal room, painted mauve, with a full wall of mirrors composing and sheer white curtains at the window that diffuse the light into the room, the wedding accessories are displayed in a tall glass cabinet. This is where the bride-to-be can present herself, in full attire, to her chaperones for approval.

The retro room displays on the walls above the dress rails a sombrero, boater, straw hat, masks and panpipes – a fancy dress wardrobe. There are plenty of handbags, belts, purses and necklaces to accessorise the chosen costume. The mantelpiece is decorated with framed postcards of museum-piece costumes and collectable 50s clocks. A montage of black and white images exemplify designers throughout the modern age, from Dior's 'New Look' to present day, bracketing the 'retro' term.

In the eveningwear room, many headscarves are tied together to form decorative bunting around the bay window. There are a large number of formal hats and accessories. Iain finds that the 'eveningwear' is marketed more successfully as 'prom' wear. He is clearly aware of the careful consideration required to maximise the shop's resources and profit, going out of his way to show me around and discuss the challenges of running the operation.

Downstairs the shop is a neat, self-respecting, traditional charity shop. A dark green carpet is offset against buttery yellow walls. The left side unit of the shop is packed with high street label clothing. There are rotating racks of greeting cards and a large glass-fronted cabinet is full of costume jewellery. Solid wooden shelves line the walls of the entrance unit, tailored to house CDs, VHS tapes of popular films that appear to be consistently outdated by about five years and a plethora of household goods, housed above a pleasingly restricted number of books. Most notable is the shop's extensive collection of Potteries chinaware, with an emphasis on presentation at the dining table. Attractive tea sets are priced at between £5 and £10. Dinner services, for the traditional British dinner, with gravy boat, look quaint against the utensils of European food culture, such as spice racks, a pestle and mortar, an elaborately tall pepper mill and an ornate ice bucket.

ADDRESS 114 Camden Road, Tunbridge Wells, Kent TELEPHONE 01892 523 206 OPEN Monday to Friday 11am - 4pm, Saturday 10am - 1pm

Wedding Belle, FARA - Surbiton, Surrey

FARA is a registered charity both in the UK and Romania and has been actively working with orphaned and abandoned children in Romania since 1991.

From the outside this outlet looks like a common charity shop, with no external advertisement for its specialist department. The customer is drawn rapidly into the heart of the long, narrow shop where, beyond a small, child-safety gate, there is a descending staircase that leads to a self-contained area dedicated to the wedding occasion. A silver helium-filled balloon in the shape of an arrow tied to the banister signposts the Wedding Belle department, directing customers down the stairs. A few choice designer outfits hang on the stairwell wall overhead. A price tag of £28 hangs exposed from a fashionable Press & Bastyan two-piece suit and heightens expectation of a high quality of stock in the basement.

Downstairs, the room is clean, airy and modern. Outfits and dresses for the wedding guests fill the rails along the left wall. An YSL fuchsia silk-organza shirt is £20. A cherry-print Moschino two-piece is £60. Familiar high end high street labels, such as Whistles and Reiss, make repeat appearances and command the same prices. Accessories for the guests are a more interesting mix of new and vintage. A 1940s leather purse handbag is simply described on its tag as 'old', in order to justify its £4 price. The pricing appears not to discriminate between the eras of manufacture and current fashions.

Wedding dresses filter into the collection towards the end of the long rail. Grooms' tailcoats congregate around a freestanding rail on the floor close by.

A three-piece suit is sensibly priced at £30. All the dresses have been reduced in price, to between £100 and £150. Original charity shop prices, crossed out with red pen, are on average twenty-five per cent more and, for the quality of fabric and detail common to the collection, this seems like a very reasonable revaluation. It is August and, browsing this quiet room, I presume that this year's brides have already bought their dresses. Whilst I speculate, a mother and daughter interrupt my solitude in the Wedding Belle boutique. The popular wedding season may be almost over but the volunteer shop assistant testifies to a steady foot-flow throughout the year of ruminating brides-to-be.

I move towards a suitably spacious dressing room, with a mirror taking up the whole wall, at the back of the room. Peeping out from behind the curtain is a large white crinoline. Several net veils hang on the back of the changing room wall, which I am told sell more frequently than the dresses. Next to them are wall-mounted shelves full of cream and white satin heels. Accessories are popular because brides tend to buy several variations to have a choice. They are also popular dressing-up garb. Under the stairs there are pageboy and bridesmaid outfits on various fancy-dress fantasy themes: the Victorian swain and the Pre-Raphaelite princess, in Dimity prints and synthetic velvet and lace.

The concentration of designer clothing downstairs suggests that the best of the shop's donations are kept for these rails. When I take some time to look at the clothes upstairs, however, I find several top labels that would otherwise suit a special occasion. Two new, identical Burberry pleated silk skirts – one in peach and the other in cream –are £35 each. An elaborately embroidered Dior Boutique jacket in navy seersucker wool is £60. A classic Perry Ellis gingham organza silk shirt and a silvery grey Maxmara shirt are both £20. They are a UK size 14, as are almost all of the garments I peruse. I come across several other brand new Maxmara pieces and so I inquire about the multiples on the rails. The manager tells me that the charity's central London shops send their surplus stock here. If any clothes have not sold in the flagship stores within two weeks of their introduction, the designer garments are reduced and then moved on to the regional shops.

Whilst she tries to keep a balanced selection of high end labels across the two floors, the manager also tries to save up the best pieces for the seasonal sales, where spending fever realises the best prices for the most valuable goods. The tactic is a successful one as the shop just recently made a reportedly significant but undisclosed sum for the charity, at the recent Summer Sale. The labels I am seeing are leftovers from that sale, indicating that a superb treasury of designer clothing is accrued for these events.

There is a range of bric-a-brac in addition to the clothing and I buy a 2008 Molskine page-a-day diary for £3 and move on to the next shop, The Fircroft Trust (see 'Music & Film').

ADDRESS 25 Victoria Road, Surbiton, Surrey KT6 4JZ TELEPHONE 020 8399 9643 OPEN Monday to Friday 9am - 5pm, Saturday 10am - 4pm

Bridal gowns in immaculate condition at St Giles, Swadlincote. ADDRESS 8
Midland Road, Swadlincote, Derbyshire DE11 0AG TELEPHONE 01283 551
591 OPEN Monday to Saturday 9:30am - 4.15pm

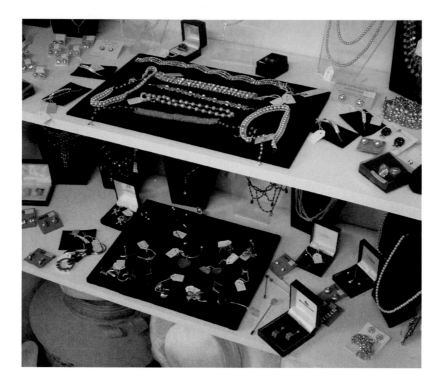

Accessories and hats at the British Red Cross, Dorking. The bridal boutique is above the BRC shop on Dorking's high street, surrounded by Box Hill and the Surrey countryside. ADDRESS 193 High Street, Dorking RH4 1RU TELEPHONE 01306 882 819 OPEN Monday to Saturday 9am - 5pm

The Bridal Room is on the first floor at Tenovus, Bristol. ADDRESS 181, Gloucester Road, Bishopston, Bristol BS7 8BG TELEPHONE 01179 427 744 OPEN Monday to Saturday 9am - 5pm

The bridal department at Oxfam, Leicester caters for traditional white weddings but also reflects Leicester's large Asian community with a collection of clothing and accessories fit for all occasions ADDRESS 22 Market Street, Leicester LE1 6DP TELEPHONE 0116 255 6425 (or 0116 255 4471) OPEN Monday to Saturday 9am - 5pm (appointments advised)

There is a modest selection of bridalwear at Sense, Margate, which also houses on the first floor a 'Bargain Books & Music' collection. ADDRESS 126 High St, Margate, Kent CT9 1JW TELEPHONE 01843 297 666 OPEN Monday to Saturday 9am - 4:30pm

Following a positive response to its wedding dress appeal last year, well over three hundred wedding dresses were donated by the public to The Big C, Norwich. The first floor has been transformed into a bridal haven that showcases an array of wedding dresses from 1950 to 2007, as well as tiaras, flowers, veils, shoes, bridesmaid dresses and outfits for the mother of the bride and the groom. ADDRESS 45 Timber Hill, Norwich, Norfolk NR1 3LA TELEPHONE 01603 761 029 OPEN Monday to Saturday 9:30am – 4:30pm

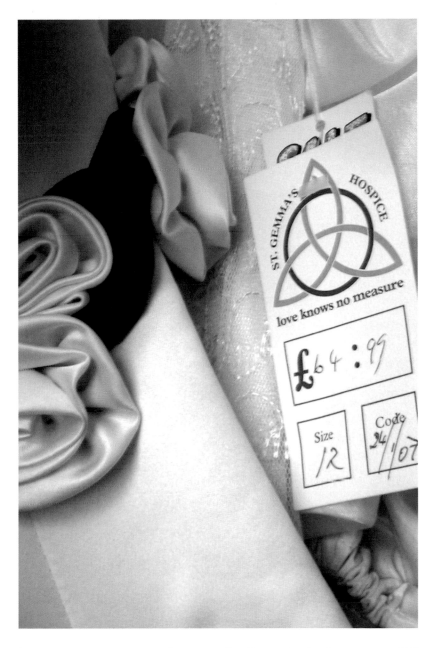

Decorative trimmings on dresses at St. Gemma's, Leeds. ADDRESS 385
Harehills Lane, Leeds LS9 6EY TELEPHONE 0113 240 5272 OPEN Monday to
Saturday 9am - 5pm

The well-preserved art deco interior at St Ann's, Cheadle (see p124).

DESIGNER

CLOTHING

Crusaid - Victoria, London

Set up in 1986 by a small group of friends, Crusaid was 'a direct response to the destructive nature of AIDS in the 1980s'. Crusaid's earliest grants were to projects such as in-patient hospital wards and helping with funeral expenses.

The original Crusaid shop opened in 1993 on Upper Tachbrook Street, but since moving to its current Churton Street site, in 1999, it has quickly gained popularity and now confidently describes itself as 'London's favourite charity shop'. It has enjoyed much press attention in recent years, with Time Out and the Telegraph Magazine both having profiled the shop in their recommendation lists. Crusaid proudly displays these articles in its window, much like many of the local restaurants advertise their accolades.

Located in SW1, the shop has enjoyed royal patronage since its inception, from nearby Kensington Palace. The shop's high class catchment has raised its calibre above that of the average charity shop. Ralph Lauren, Nicole Farhi and EMI have all shown their support by making repeated donations, but equally valuable are the personal contributions from local residents. Donated goods are of a consistently high quality and an abundance of moneyed local customers means that the shop can demand high prices to match. Crusaid has also become a destination shop for those prepared to make a special trip to shop, inspired both by the publicity and word of mouth amongst keen charity shoppers. The degree to which charity shopping has become a hobbyist activity seems to be comparable with the popularity of 'car-booting' as a pastime, with insider information circulated amongst those 'in the know'. This enterprise does not appear to excessively exploit its coveted status, working on the principles of a fast turnover rather than achieving the very top prices. 'The business is based on kindness and generosity,' says its website. It is, of course, a business and focused on making money but it feels to me like the charity does manage to strike a good balance between profit-making and the provision of affordable goods for the London public.

There are a lot of designer labels on the rails of this small, well-stocked shop, because of benefactors like Roger Walker Dack, Alan Clarke, and Juicy Couture. Nicole Farhi gives generously every couple of months to this establishment and the shop has developed a reputation for its famous, fashion-linked donors because evidence of their donations can be found on the rails at any given time. A Farhi top costs about £10. There are plenty of designer men's suits for around £100. Due to the nature of the charity, and uncommon to most charity shops, men are catered for in clothing as much as women.

Celebrity customers are happy to associate themselves as customers with this charity shop. Alan Carr calls it 'the Harvey Nichols of charity shops'. David Collins is quoted on the website as saying 'I donate on a regular basis. It's the ethical thing to do.' The drummer from 90s pop band Blur, Dave Rowntree, has signed the changing room wall, alongside several other famous names.

Crusaid has a good reputation for music and, before Christmas, the record label EMI donated more than 1,000 jazz CDs. There are several framed, collectors' 7" singles decorating one wall, to whet the appetite of the discerning vinyl hunter. There is a decent book and record selection in 'The Library' room at the back of the shop, incorporating an extensive gay section as well as the usual categories. The room looks like a set for a bohemian-styled World Of Interiors shoot. A chandelier creates a web of shimmering shadows on the ceiling. There is a generously proportioned wooden chair, adorned with a draped tassle-shawl and luxurious cushions, where customers are offered a seat next to an antique dressing table, under natural light from the large-scale rear window, to browse through the books. This is a league away from the strip-lights of most charity shops.

Outside the front of the shop there is a selection of bric-a-brac and bargains, in clean, clear plastic boxes, to draw in the passer-by. Peering in through the window and I see exactly what I have been looking out for – a 8mm film projector – on sale for a reasonable £15. At the till counter I am assured that all electrical goods are checked before they are put out on display and so I can be sure that this one will work safely.

ADDRESS 19 Churton Street, London SW1V 2LY TELEPHONE 020 7233 8736 OPEN Monday to Saturday 10am - 6pm Sunday 11am - 3pm

British Red Cross - Chelsea, London

The BRC is a volunteer-led humanitarian organisation that helps people in crisis.

The Chelsea BRC shop is located on Old Church Street, relating to the charity's historical occupation of church-owned premises. Having undergone refurbishment in early 2008, doubling its former size, the shop has been refitted with modern lighting, flooring and a new shop front. Not only has the shop extended its original floor space by incorporating the ground floor sorting room but it has also acquired a smaller unit next door, which is accessed separately from the street, combining two specialist outlets side-by-side.

The main unit sells high quality vintage and designer clothing and accessories. Loyal customers and special guests were invited to the launch of the refurbished shop for the privileged preview of an even bigger collection of designer clothing, shoes and accessories. Subsequently 'designer evenings' have been hosted throughout the year, the last event raising £20,000 for the BRC in just three hours. Any donated pieces that are deemed particularly special are held back for the benefit of these evenings. The shop describes itself as 'a popular second-hand shop', which suggests to me that it competes with the private sector in an area of London renowned since the 1960s for its cutting-edge fashion and antiques dealers.

The shop receives its precious fashion pieces in regular donations from wealthy Chelsea residents as well as from top designers themselves. Labels such as Vivienne Westwood, Nicole Farhi and Smythson are commonplace because the designers' studios are local and they give generously to the shop, keeping it well-stocked with highly saleable goods. The fact that the residents and donors are also customers and are willing to spend a lot of money here makes it possible for only the best items to be put out on the shop floor, so a consistently high quality of stock is maintained which encourages visitors to return.

Manager Cathy Shimmel has a long history in fashion herself, working for Catherine Walker and Biba previously. She is stylishly dressed and talks to the customers in a confident and relaxed manner, happy to offer her expert advice. She extracts individual garments for my attention as she thinks they might suit me, and describes the qualities of the clothes that she picks out with an intimate knowledge. Cathy tells me that she does not like to put out low or even mid-range labels like Marks & Spencer but makes an exception for Jigsaw because it is made with some quality, which exemplifies the lowest standard of high street fashion available in this shop. 'Tom Ford's studio is around the corner and his boys come in to look at the detail and finishing on some of our vintage clothes,' says Cathy. There is an uncommonly large proportion of genuine vintage wear here, indiscriminately mixed in with contemporary garments (this shop could easily have been included in the 'Vintage' section of this book).

Whilst browsing the rails, the young shop assistant approaches to ask me if I would like any help and, once I have loaded my arms with items to try on, she offers to put them in the changing room for me so that I can continue shopping. This is a professional style of service unusual to the charity shop experience. The financial success of this shop affords it a strata of paid staff in addition to its managerial position, attracting and enabling young people to join the sector. I ask the assistant if she is able to enjoy the perk of first-pickings on donations that come in. She points out a bracelet that she has had her eye on but explains that all items must be put out on the shop floor for a mandatory forty-eight hours before staff or volunteers are allowed to purchase them.

I notice that there are no overcoats on the rails. It is June and all clothes on the rails are geared towards the summer. When I ask if this is a natural pattern in terms of donations the assistant offers to bring out some coats from the stockroom for me to try on. Clothes that are considered irrelevant to the current British season are put aside, where possible, for sale at a later date. The best examples are of course saved for the designer evenings, I am told. The girl brings down an immaculate vintage linen coat, which ties at the waist, fully lined and with edges bound in a stiff cotton velvet. A modern jacquard full-length dress coat with a vintage feel and a Marc Jacobs take on a traditional pea coat are in mint condition and priced at around £100.

Next door the old stock room is now the subsidiary bric-a-brac and book shop. Again, the level of quality here is top-notch. There is a comprehensive selection of household goods that is given an overall 'collectable' sheen by a smattering of antique curios, such as leather-cased tape measures and boules. A large amount of art is donated to the shop, forming an 'amateur artists' area. As with the clothing department, there are regular art sales events, by invitation, at the shop every couple of months, I have just missed the most recent art sale but I look over some attractive leftovers. One watercolour that is almost abstracted by its simplicity, with a horizon dividing the canvas equally into two parts, sea and sky, and with dimensions measuring approximately 170 x 270mm within its frame, is priced at £70. I am told that the artist's signed name, C.H. Drummond, is 'in the book', meaning that the artist has been recognised in collectors' guides. A pair of contemporary graphite-stick drawings, scored out of a sketchbook, although not framed, is priced at £20.

Despite being able to employ staff, the shop still relies on volunteers to fill the gap. Oscar Eavis volunteers in the shop in his spare time. Also a loyal customer, he and his family visit the shop without fail every week to snap up the latest designer goods. 'I say to my friends I shop at the "Croix Rouge Boutique", he says. 'I don't need to shop anywhere else and it's great knowing that my money is going to the Red Cross, which does such a good job.'

ADDRESS 69-71 Old Church Street, London SW3 5BS TELEPHONE 020 7376 7300 OPEN Monday to Saturday 10:30am - 6pm. From March, Sunday 12pm - 6pm (closed Sunday in winter).

Cancer Research - Marylebone, London

Cancer Research helps to raise funds to look after people with cancer as well as funding research into the treatment of cancer.

This shop has recently had a re-fit and looks fresh and spacious, although it is also more like the generic corporate face of a national chain. It is refreshing to see that the charity has refrained from styling its lucrative flagship store in the bohemian chic that pervades the city's 'on trend' bars as well as fashion boutiques and now speciality charity shops also. Instead, Cancer Research has expanded its available floor space, refurbishing with standard strip pine flooring and chrome shop fittings that allow the clothes to hang airily on the rails.

This shop currently takes more money per unit than any other charity shop in the country. Marylebone is one of the smartest regions of London and its high street has a distinctly local feel, providing for the daily living of its residents, albeit with goods at the very top of the range. The shop enjoys a lot of local traffic and as donations are mostly top quality designer wear, prices are high. However, as manager Natasha points out, the value of an item here is only what someone is prepared to pay for it, and there are enough regular clients to this shop who are able and willing to pay a premium.

The Highgate branch, with another wealthy catchment, also attracts impressive donations regularly, but it is unable to achieve the same prices for its goods. An Alexander McQueen jacket that was recently donated to Highgate could not be expected to reach more than about £100, whereas Marylebone took the garment and sold it for £300. Even at that price it only stayed on the rails for four days. The average price for garments here is £25 whereas at the Camden branch (See 'Retro & Vintage'), for example, it is only £4. Marylebone returns the favour other shops have paid it by sending to Camden any generic retro pieces it receives and to Highgate any excess quality high street labels (this also preserves some consistency of stock).

A shop with a reputation for a certain type or quality of goods takes on a distinctive character and a momentum of its own. That 'like attracts like' is recognised by this collective of Cancer Research shops, to optimise the fundraising potential of each. The idea is that customers whose experience of the shop has been consistent over a number of years will always make a special trip to shop here, supplementing its loyal local custom. Competing with the spending power of local residents may put the most desirable labels out of reach for many charity shoppers, but the reductions keep them far below their original pricetags.

YSL, Gucci and Burberry are commonly seen on the rails, alongside the more avant-garde silhouettes of Issey Miyake and *Comme Des Garcons* and younger names such as Bernhardt Wilhelm, of which I buy an elastic structured skirt for £15. An Issey Miyake Pleats Please dress is £45 and a full-length dress coat is twice that price. A pale gold satin Versace body-con dress is £40 and two YSL layered silk skirts are £200 a-piece, all notably unworn. One week later when I visit the shop again all of these items have gone. There are now several new Philip Treacy hats, donated by the milliner himself, and several new Nicole Farhi items. It strikes me that the majority of labels and prices here are equitable with TKMaxx stores. There is a particularly good selection of shoes, including Miu Miu boots for £70 and a pair of Stella McCartney suede heels for £80, both with negligible wear to the soles.

Today the manager points out that the shop is low on stock. 'The more people become familiar with the Internet and auction sites such as eBay, the less they will want to give away their valuables and the more our prices will be will levelled by that,' she says. She goes on to describe the moment of opening a donation bag. If the first thing she pulls out is good then the rest tends to be of comparable quality, she tells me, and this can sustain the shop for a week. A recent celebrity dress auction by hairstylist James Brown, who lost two sisters to cancer, has made the shop the subject of much recent press. Natasha can see very clearly the impact of celebrity endorsements and press publicity, which immediately result in a sudden gust of donations of a higher quality. The shop must sustain a high profile if it is to maintain decent stock and keep up with the innovations of its charity competitors.

Cancer Research has recently joined forces with eco-couture designers Revamp to launch in the Marylebone shop, exclusively amongst the charity shops, a collection of garments and accessories reworked from recycled stock. The range showcases the best in established and emerging design talent from across the United Kingdom. There is an abundance of designs, from floral print dresses to trinket jewellery pieces, and each item has been carefully handcrafted into something unique. Through this partnership, the charity aims to highlight the ecological benefits of reclaimed and vintage fashions, to lessen the environmental impact of the industry. The initiative was introduced at around the same time Oxfam launched its Sustainable Boutiques in the city and complements the charity's drive to be actively and visibly more environmentally sound. Items can also be purchased online from its eBay site. Fifty per cent of profits goes towards the charity's cause.

Natasha is happy to allow more space in the shop for the launch of this new label, for the time being, whilst donated stocks are down. She has worked by trial and error together with Revamp to establish the right selection to sell successfully in the shop. Interestingly, at first the clothes were too high end and resisted sale at prices that were above average for this shop, but they now level out at the £35 mark and the range is doing much better. There is a small window for prices that the average customer is prepared to pay and the shop aims to provide as many goods as possible to fit that range.

ADDRESS 24 Marylebone High Street, London W1U 4PQ TELEPHONE 020 7487 4986 OPEN Monday to Saturday 10am - 6pm, Sunday 11am - 5pm

Marie Curie - Richmond, Surrey

Marie Curie provides free nursing care to cancer patients and those with other terminal illnesses in their own homes.

The Marie Curie in Richmond is a small but well-stocked shop on the corner of the Lichfield Court, a listed 1930s housing development on Lichfield Terrace in the town centre. With the sun reflecting brightly off the white-stuccoed walls of the apartment block, the little corner window of the shop with its delicate wooden frame painted the Marie Curie cobalt blue shows off to great effect an array of pressed glassware and costume jewellery.

This is a charity shop already well-known for its designer labels and quality bric-a-brac that reflect the wealthy demographic of the area. The mannequin in the main front window is dressed in a women's black Armani two-piece skirt suit, for £60. In the shop this figure stands back-to-back with another, sporting a men's double-breasted Hugo Boss suit for the same price. This amount appears to be a standard price for the shop's most prized clothing. Hanging behind the till - around which the charity shop tends to retain its most valuable stock - is a quilted, emerald-green silk David Emmanuel two-piece women's suit and 'a pair of new G-Star jeans', as the price tag identifies them. Both items are marked at £60 also. Prevalent price tag descriptions attached to the merchandise indicate that garments are pre-sorted and their value carefully calculated in an attempt to justify the cost to customers.

For a small shop there is a lot of stock on offer and yet the space does not feel overcrowded, even though there are several other customers browsing the rails when I visit. I am told by the manager that the clothing ought to be colour-coordinated, according to the charity's retailing guidelines, although I am happy that he has not got around to doing so yet. His time is instead almost entirely occupied by pricing and putting out the stock. I find a good range of womenswear labels here, all from the top end of the high street shops, dominated by Monsoon, Jigsaw, Viyella and contemporary Jaeger. Max

& Co. and Ronit Zilka bear the highest prices, hovering at around £20 for a top. I am impressed by the more realistically priced black court shoes by Patrick Cox and a Tula handbag, both in excellent condition and priced at £22 and £12 respectively. These are set amongst an overall decent selection of women's shoes and accessories. The best buy in the womenswear section is a vintage Janis Wainwright (of 47 Poland Street) black wool two-piece skirt suit with elegantly embroidered detail on the jacket – an attractive buy if it had not been in an inconceivably small size, which may explain the reasonable price of £35. When I venture to return it to its place on the rails, a shop assistant volunteer intervenes and offers to show me how best to do so.

The menswear range is more impressive with many designer men's suits on offer, all in average sizes and perfect condition. A beautifully made Kenzo suit jacket is £12.99 and there are several Hugo Boss two-pieces for not much more. Looking through the vinyl records, in storage boxes on the floor beneath, I see an EP by Mick Jagger who is a local resident and also a regular patron, the volunteer confirms. The shop has several celebrity donors living locally who give regularly enough that the high level of quality brands I encounter on my visit represents accurately a staple proportion of the stock.

The art that is on sale here is an equally noteworthy collection, which fills the walls of the changing room and decorates the shop, overcoming the restrictions on space and readily catching the eye. My attention is drawn to one crude and curious painting in particular, depicting a robed skeleton, a set of playing cards, a bi-plane, an old-fashioned motorcar and spy figure with brief case, mysteriously grouped together against an aged and mottled brown background, with gilt frame. There is a fifty per cent sale on all artwork but, despite the dexterity in its execution, its kitsch value does not quite justify its £55 price tag for me.

ADDRESS 1 Lichfield Terrace, Sheen Road, Richmond, Surrey TW9 1AS
TELEPHONE 020 8940 1800 OPEN Monday - Saturday 9:30am - 5pm

FARA - Parsons Green, London

Actively working with orphaned and abandoned children in Romania since 1991.

This is a small shop situated amidst a short stretch of shops at Parsons Green, on the New Kings Road. Next door is a consignment dress agency, called *Deuxieme*, that sells 'laundered and fashionable designer and vintage wear' on commission. The co-owner of *Deuxieme* tells me that a lot of their clothes end up 'next door' if they fail to sell after eight weeks, so their shop offers a last chance for customers to recoup some money before the clothes are donated to charity. Whether goods end up here by default or because local residents actively choose to take last season's wardrobe straight to FARA, the shop is full of desirable specimens of designer labels from the more unusual Prada designs to the more conservative, classic Feraud suits.

The top shelves of the shop are lined with boutique carrier bags denoting the type of clothes stocked in the shop, and the changing room is lined with the pages of top-end fashion magazines. An antique Singer sewing machine features in the top-shelf display, set up as if in mid-alteration of a garment and suggesting that any items on sale might simply require a bit of home alteration – a button replaced or a hem taken up – to be restored to their immaculate condition. The customer is then reminded that they are presented with the opportunity to purchase a top label at a bargain price.

Deuxieme claims that it is able to sell cashmere for less than its FARA neighbour but the charity shop only prices items for as much as it is able to sell them, which perhaps indicates that customers are prepared to pay over the odds for the sake of charity. Overall, the prices are not bad and many of them have been marked down by fifty per cent in red pen on the label, in order to keep stock moving. Garments are also circulated around the other FARA shops nearby if, for some reason, they remain on the rails for too long.

The back section of the shop looks over a small courtyard garden, with a sofa in front of the window, displaying men's clothes. A framed selection of old postcards from abroad and a leather briefcase placed above the shoe rack reflect in kitsch fashion the profile of its cosmopolitan male customer. The suits are all recognisable designer labels and in mint condition. Two-piece suits are priced at between £45 and £85. I suspect that this takes into consideration the fact that men are not generally prepared to spend as much on fashion, as these prices seem disproportionate to those in the women's section. There is also access, in this part of the shop, to the lower ground floor that doubles the retail space.

The basement of the shop is full of bric-a-brac. A giant cardboard cut-out of Marilyn Monroe greets me at the bottom of the stairs, as part of a still-life arrangement of props that include a large travelling trunk, sets of golf clubs and balls, fake flowers in random receptacles that have been re-appropriated as vases and sit on top of a few pieces of wooden furniture. A delicately proportioned side table is £35. A wicker basket chair is £30. There are sets of lined, floral chintz curtains for around £45. Along the length of one wall

are shelves full of crockery, including a large amount of Poole Pottery, hand-painted ceramic chicken pots and upmarket kitchenware. There is also a small book section that appears to consist mostly of hardback biographies.

I am most interested in the large amount of framed canvas paintings that are available, adding to the already significant number displayed in the front window of the shop. On this particular occasion, the artwork has all been donated by a single benefactor who has signed the pictures with a curious symbol. There is a combination of life and still-life painting, which reminds me that Kensington and Chelsea College is situated nearby and that this is historically an artistic area. The assistant confirms that the shop often receives donations of paintings from local artists clearing out their studios. It consistently receives a large selection of original amateur and professional artworks.

ADDRESS 297 New King's Road, London, SW6 4RE TELEPHONE 020 7736 2833 OPEN Monday to Saturday 10am - 6pm Sunday 11am - 5pm

BARK - Berwick-upon-Tweed, Northumberland

Berwick Animal Rescue Kennels is a registered charity whose aim is to provide a rescue and re-homing service for stray and unwanted domestic animals throughout north Northumberland and Berwickshire.

Berwick has many charity shops along its main high street, from the top end, where painter LS Lowry portrayed many views of the town, to the bottom end by the buttermarket at the back of the Guildhall, where this small, traditional charity shop is located. There is a regular and balanced mix of goods on sale here, although children's clothing takes up an entire rail along one side, all bearing good quality labels. Both the menswear and womenswear rails that divide the centre of the shop contain a large amount of knitwear, which is unsurprising in this North East climate and represents the Scottish Borders' history of wool production and the manufacture of tweed and hosiery.

Many of the sweaters in the B.A.R.K. charity shop are unworn and there are several collections in the same style, with the occasional cashmere piece. There are many distinguished luxury brands, the most prominent of which is Pringle, known for its classic sporting identity. I choose two Pringle sweaters from a collection of three signature argyles with an appliquéd golfing motif. Despite their outdated design they are brand new.

Founded in 1815 in the Scottish Borders, the Pringle Company was once the biggest employer in Berwick until it shut its factory there in 1998.

All production moved to the founding factory site in Hawick, creating overnight unemployment for many of the town's resident workers. Dawson International, who owns the Pringle brand, was criticised heavily for what was perceived to be the result of an overly rapid expansion policy, leaving the residents of Berwick feeling an enormous sense of betrayal. 'The Berwick people were so angry that they didn't want to wear the sweaters anymore and we got a lot donated. We still do, from time to time,' one volunteer tells me. The once popular label, also indigenous to the local culture, is now unanimously discarded.

Accounting for the regular supply of other luxury knitwear in the charity shop is the local Mill Warehouse, which sells factory seconds and often donates end-of-sale stock, such as Derrick Rose. Garments of this class, however, have gradually been eclipsed at The Mill by cheaper products manufactured overseas. Under economic conditions that have presented insurmountable obstacles for all exporting companies in the small rural town, the Borders knitwear industry has suffered massively and the charity shop seems to be, at present, collecting the fallout of goods from this decline and at the same time fulfilling a practical function in offering the opportunity for thrifty purchases to locals. With no personal, emotional links to a key local industry undergoing radical changes, my purchases are the windfall of a tourist charity shopper, although I suspend wearing them for the time I am in Berwick.

ADDRESS BARK, 12 Church Street, Berwick-upon-Tweed, Northumberland TD15 TELEPHONE 01289 309 225 OPEN Monday to Saturday 10am - 4pm

In store displays at FARA, Fulham Road – the original FARA charity shop. It offers a wide range of clothing with a consistently high proportion of high-end designerwear. New stock is carefully selected from the large volume of donations the shop receives. Exceptional bric-a-brac, pictures and books further enhance the shop's reputation. ADDRESS 841 Fulham Road, London SW6 5HQ TELEPHONE 020 7371 0141 OPEN Monday to Saturday 10am - 6pm, Sundays 11am - 5pm

The quaint shop front of RSPCA, Wooler. On the occasion of my visit there are many high-end designer labels on the rails and I buy a pair of purple Voyage trousers, a narrative print Ana Sui dress and a Jasper Conran silk blouse, all for under £40. ADDRESS 28-32 High Street, Wooler, Northumberland NE7 6EF TELEPHONE 01668 282400 2833 OPEN Monday to Saturday 10am - 4pm in the summer and 10am - 3pm in the winter. Closed Thursday.

Previously known as The Notting Hill Housing Trust, the charity has retained and renamed its Kings Road shop as 'Octavia' – one of nineteen throughout London. ADDRESS 303 Kings Road, London SW3 5EP TELEPHONE 020 7736 2833 OPEN Monday to Saturday 10am - 6pm, Sunday 12pm - 5pm

Located on the busy pedestrian shopping street, George Street, which has become a reputable charity shop run, Hove YMCA has a 'famous brands' rail and retro area. ADDRESS 26 George Street, Hove, East Sussex BN3 3YA TELEPHONE 01273 749 139 OPEN Monday to Saturday 9am - 5pm

At the British Red Cross shop in the heart of Belgravia (one of London's most expensive areas), a quick thumb through the racks reveals an Armani men's suit for £80, Gucci shoes for £25, Abercrombie & Fitch jeans for £25 and Ralph Lauren sandals for £30. Vintage items can sometimes be found here as well. ADDRESS 81 Ebury Street, Victoria, London, SW1W 9QU TELEPHONE 020 7730 2235 OPEN Monday to Friday 10am - 5:40pm, Saturday 10am - 4pm

Revamp branding at Cancer Research, Marylebone (see page 148).

A bright interior at the British Red Cross, Chelsea (see page 146).

EMPORIUM

Civic Amenity Site, Hove YMCA
- Hove, East Sussex

Hove YMCA charity shops are a vital way of generating
income for the YMCA's work amongst the community and
'offer a home for all those unwanted gifts'.

The amenity site near the Old Shoreham Road is the council tip where
residents can take household waste for recycling and disposal. Viola – one
of the UK's largest recycling and waste management companies – rent a
warehouse space on site to Hove YMCA, so that it can set itself up as an
intervention facility for the reuse of goods brought to the tip by the public.
The charity has committed to a lease of five years, with rates and overheads
included in the price, during which time it will be bound by Viola's rules on
site. As they drive up to the tip, all visitors must pass the warehouse, which
identifies itself as a 'charity shop' by a sign above the door.

YMCA staff are happy to accept anything visitors dump that might be
saleable, especially furniture and electrical goods, which they check before
selling on. PAT testing is conducted on site, on all appliances, and the YMCA
electrical shop on Blatchington Road (see 'Electrical') employs technicians
who are able to carry out worthwhile repairs. Like any regular charity shop the
amenity site shop is restricted by fire regulations in what it can sell on, but it
has the space to take in, display and store larger pieces of furniture as well as
other items that may require particular attention before they are fit for re-sale.
The shop promotes itself by citing the ethics of charitable giving and recycling
to protect the environment.

Previously, goods discarded by the public that were fit for reuse were
commonly (although unofficially) profiteered by the tip workers, rather than
squandered, but new regulations have put a stop to such activity. Viola staff
are now able to redirect anyone with quality goods for disposal to the YMCA
warehouse, ensuring that unwanted, functioning goods are conserved and
that a good cause will benefit.

Everything that is sold from the site shop is logged and the charity's targets
are assessed by weight. There is a weighbridge at the access point to the site
and weekly weight records chart the charity's progress. YMCA vans are the
only vehicles to exit the site heavier than they were when they entered, having
loaded up goods from the warehouse to distribute throughout the Hove
shops, wherever suitable. Some items do not sell well at the site. There is a
'tip mentality', I am told by the staff, such that people are not prepared to
pay high prices for goods that they so closely associate with landfill waste.
The high street charity shops can achieve better prices for most of the goods
brought in here.

The charity's finance department refers to an official weight list in order
to appraise the shop's targets. It is estimated that an average of six tonnes
each month, in electrics and bric-a-brac alone, leave the site, in four van
loads each week. Including furniture, four hundred tonnes is thought to be a

conservative estimate of how much landfill is redirected by this venture each year. At present there is no tax credit for landfill in the region.

Despite keeping the YMCA shops in good stock, the warehouse still retains an impressive selection of items for sale. Two long scaffolding trestles run down the length of the unit and present an unusual and immediately striking jungle of plants, donated in their plastic pots and many now transferred to decorative ceramic pots. There are flowering orchids and tomato plants that have been nurtured into fruit by the staff. The greenery is complimented by a large selection of garden furniture. Deckchairs and large luggage trunks offer theatrical styles for garden dwellers.

Household furniture takes up the majority of the remaining space. Chests of drawers are lined up along the floor underneath the leafy rows of plants. The staff discusses the current vogue in furniture sales; two years ago re-production corner units would have fetched £70 but trade has changed and now the staff feel lucky to achieve £30 for the same pieces. 'Vintage IKEA' is currently very popular, they tell me. For further collections, YMCA furniture shops are located on London Road, in the heart of Brighton's reviving market area, and Blatchington Road in Hove.

Wall mounted shelving and bookcases are full of books, videos and DVDs, selling at 50p and £1 respectively. Small selections of disparate objects have naturally accumulated in the corners of the space; a bookcase of car manuals and an almost full range of garden tools are the more practical finds. Alternatively, a charity collection box, in the form of a disabled boy, now politically obsolete, is hoped to fetch £5 for its kitsch or nostalgia value. There are walking sticks and trampolines, at very reasonable prices. Pictures that include many original artworks are stacked up on the floor against the wall. A selection, mounted in frames, is hung around the walls. Oil on canvas has, up to now, held its price of around £25 to £30, but 'Chinese copies of original artworks have affected the market,' one member of staff comments. The Hove YMCA is achieving notably less money per artwork than it has done at any time in the past.

There are plenty of practical DIY materials available, such as boxes of tiles that provide enough to tile a small bathroom or kitchen, as well as matching rolls of wallpaper. Adult bikes range in price from £25 to £75. There is also a selection of children's bikes selling for proportionately less, although prices are knowingly optimistic. It is illegal to increase prices once they have been set and so it makes sense to put a high price on goods with a view to reducing it if the items do not initially sell. The staff are allowed a discount on the value of goods that come in to the warehouse but they describe a 'chocolate factory syndrome' that quells their appetite for anything but the very best or that which they seek after in particular. Managers also have targets to reach, representing a Limited Trading Company for the YMCA.

ADDRESS Hove Amenity Site, Leighton Road, Hove BN3 7EL TELEPHONE 01273 321 660 OPEN Monday to Friday 8.30am - 4.30pm, Saturday 8.30am - 1.30pm

Green House, Guild Care - East Worthing, East Sussex

Guild Care provides Residential Care Homes for the Elderly, Home Care and Intermediate Care, Carers Services and Healthy Living Centre provide extensive resources for communities in Worthing and West Sussex.

A light industrial warehouse in a barren trading estate near the sea front in Worthing houses this charity superstore. A continuous pale blue screen runs around the inside perimeter in a giant curve, providing usable wall space for the retail area and creating a Green House 'stage' to imaginatively present its wares. Giant white clouds, cut out of MDF in cartoon profile are suspended from the roof, between the lights, and an inner circle of theatrical flats are painted with simple green hills, defining a furniture area. Two green painted platforms on either side of the space create islands of interest, with a geodesic dome greenhouse on each that provides a further novel and intimate setting for the smaller items of bric-a-brac. Green metal doweling sprouts out of the floor and clamps colourful pictures and postcards of flowers at its tips. These areas create a pathway around them, continuing to guide visitors around a natural environment recreated in rough ironmongery and junk.

Guild Care received lottery funding in 2003 to revamp the warehouse, with a view to pushing the principles 'Reuse, Recycle, Reduce'. Behind the scenes of this vast showroom, the Green House encompasses storage space and workshops. Guild Care has a history of innovative recycling enterprise. Its Furniture Recycling Project was set up in 1978 with a view to restoring donated furniture and electrical goods and passing them on to local people in need, or selling the goods to raise money for the charity. The restoration workshop has now been in operation for eleven years, and volunteers, some with learning difficulties, are trained by a skilled tutor in the art of restoring and repairing furniture and upholstering.

The charity shop officially builds into its programme multiple responsibilities, firstly to its parent charity, and then to local people in need, providing them with a cheap source of essential goods, and creating training and employment opportunities. Tackling environmental issues represents the collective interests of all involved. The FRP makes a significant contribution each year to waste reduction as well as social renewal in Worthing. Preventing reusable goods from being thrown away is particularly pertinent to West Sussex, which is rapidly running out of landfill space.

Educational zones are incorporated in to the design of the shop, to promote environmental awareness. There is an interactive exhibition and a library. Visitors are encouraged to impart unconventional and resourceful household tips and treatments, on notes that are pinned to a doweling tree. Practical information is provided to explain the council's recycling policies, where to recycle in the local area and how to identify recyclable household waste.

Visitors are invited to informal lectures and discussions on relevant subjects. Most importantly, the Green House encourages people to believe that they can make a difference by modifying their lifestyles, offering a sustainable community enterprise, as well as a family-friendly shopping experience.

The remaining space is divided between several departments, expanding on the regions of interest in a conventional small-scale charity shop. Each unit is presented along the route of visitor traffic and partitioned from the next by random shelving units. In the 'Collectors' Corner' there are curiosities and antiques as well as more popular items of collectable memorabilia and souvenirs, including a large number of coupon purchases from familiar household brands. I buy two identical McVitie's Rich Tea biscuits mugs. Architectural salvage items such as fireplaces are on sale at around £75. A pair of 1930s cast-iron bath feet in a simple and attractive design cost £20 and a selection of ceramic bed warmers are £5 each, along with a flat-iron.

There is no obvious pricing psychology applied here. Purbeck and Royal Doulton fetch £1.50 a cup and saucer and hand-crafted 'primula' ceramics cost £3.50 for a dish. Alfred Meakin plates and saucers are £5.99. These are all displayed in a delicate 1940s display cabinet that I am told no-one wanted to buy until it was used for displaying the antique china and now it is continually enquired after, although it is no longer for sale. A 10th Anniversary Nat King Cole LP places these eclectic items firmly in the nostalgia zone. Boiled wool blankets cushion a display of dolls and toys on top of two large packing trunks set out on the floor. There are many 'Philmar' series jigsaws. A Brexton Bakelite picnic hamper set is priced at £10. A replica blunderbuss, 'circa 1780', is £25.

In the book section, there are a number of contemporary hardback reference books on graphic design, product design and crafts. There is also a clothing section for men and women, but bric-a-brac pads out the rest of the shop in vast quantity, from charity shop clichés such as Toby jugs and flying ducks to a collection of life size 'movie' cutouts which are new to the shop.

The main focus of interest is the large collection of furniture that congregates in the middle of the space. There is a mix of the traditional and modern. Some items are renovated or decorated in the workshops, producing unique pieces. Around the furniture a low display shelf has been built for the presentation of small electrical appliances. Donated white goods and electricals are tested for safety by an accredited PAT tester as well as being checked to meet the shop's own quality standards, and are guaranteed for three months.

An electric van costs around £1 a day to run and collects unwanted furniture of reasonable quality from households in Worthing and the surrounding area, demonstrating, by example, an alternative to fossil fuels. There is a small fee for deliveries. Staff keep an eye out for individual wish lists.

ADDRESS The Green House, Meadow Road, East Worthing, West Sussex BN11 2SA TELEPHONE 01903 205 302 OPEN Monday to Saturday 9:30am - 4:30pm

Re:Store Warehouse, East Belfast Mission - Ballymacarrett, Belfast

The EBM organisation offers a range of services to meet the needs of children and young people, the homeless and unemployed and also the elderly and families in the local community. The charity aims to care for the local people from 'birth to death'.

East Belfast Mission was founded in 1985 to engage in community development and service in the Ballymacarrett district of Belfast. The aim of the Social Economy Department within EBM is to sell goods, such as good quality, nearly new clothes and furniture to local people and to reinvest profits back into the community by funding many of the Mission's programmes. There are two shops, both situated on the Newtownards Road, close to the main EBM building and the church. One is a typical charity shop selling second-hand clothes, books and bric-a-brac and the other is a very large warehouse, believed to be the largest charity shop in Ireland, selling mainly second-hand furniture.

The Re:Store warehouse has a sales floor of approximately twelve thousand square feet and houses a storage area and offices upstairs. When the leasing period came to an end in 2005, EBM decided to close its small furniture shop, further down Newtownards Road, and transform a former Cash & Carry warehouse that it owned along the same commercial stretch into a unique furniture 'store'. The local community did not particularly welcome the changes propelled by the move. Some of the regular customers felt that the new site was too big and too business-like. The main issue of contention was that the public had previously been able to pay for the goods in instalments. Whilst this policy was not entirely dropped, the warehouse insisted that the goods must be paid for in full before leaving the premises. In the smaller shop the goods were often delivered prior to full payment, which left much debt upon closure that was never recovered.

The warehouse, along with the other charity shops, sells donated items only. Donations are collected by a branded van, incorporating the slogan 'Reduce, Reuse, Recycle'. Goods purchased in the shop can be delivered but payment is required for this service, to cover fuel and running costs. Re-conditioned white goods are sold on behalf of Bryson Charitable Group, at very reasonable prices, all guaranteed for six months. Furniture to suit every need is grouped together in general areas of interest throughout the space. There are beds and bedroom furniture, small occasional furniture, electrical goods, dining room furniture, books and bric-a-brac. Soft furnishings such as curtains and small rugs occupy rails in a corner region of the shop. There is a specified music area selling LPSs, CDs and DVDs and good quality toys and games are sold only in 'nearly new' condition.

As a social enterprise, EBM aims to fulfil the 'triple bottom line'. This means that it hopes to achieve social, financial and environmental goals within its community. In order to raise money and regenerate profits through its partnerships with social care organisations, it welcomes private customers and landlords, as well as crews purchasing goods for film sets, from outside of the local area. The charity will shortly be trading items of interest on eBay.

Such a diverse and large scale operation engages the workforce in many different ways. EBM is one of the largest community organisations in the area, with its charity shops providing employment, student placements and volunteering opportunities for local people and fulfilling its Social Economy programme, including its Stepping Stones employability programme. EBM mobilises a staff team of fifty and a volunteer team of more than seventy people in the service of the community.

Many workers are also members of the church congregation who enjoy serving the public and appreciate the opportunity for conversation, often personally familiar with the customers. Some like to carry out administration or operate the till and others prefer to operate the loading bay or travel in the van to assist with furniture collections and deliveries. A large proportion of volunteers are long term unemployed, people who have returned to work after many years of perhaps raising a family or those with mental health problems or lacking confidence who are looking to gain new skills. EBM believes that by addressing social issues it keeps its volunteers on board. It involves itself in any personal matters that people may bring with them, offering help with benefit entitlements, pastoral advice and counselling, or practical provisions such as warm clothing for the winter. A hot meal is supplied to any volunteer who works a full day in any of the projects.

By emphasising its environmental concerns, such as recycling and waste issues, the charity aims to encourage people to think about what they throw away and to carefully consider whether their waste could be resold. Re:Store works in close partnership with the local councils to remove bulky waste items that are reusable, to sell in the shops. Financial assistance from the Community Waste Innovation Fund has enabled EBM to further develop its charity shops under the 'Recycle and Resale of Furniture and Electrical Goods' project. As part of this initiative it has received funding to develop three new furniture stores, in North Street, in the centre of Belfast and in Larne and Antrim, which are serviced by two further branded vans. Since the opening in Larne earlier this year, the charity has already intercepted and diverted over a tonne of waste from the waste stream. EBM now operates a total of five charity shops, all trading under the name Re:Store, and plans to expand its fundraising business and broaden its community.

ADDRESS East Belfast Mission, 241 Newtownards Road, Belfast BT4 1AF
TELEPHONE 028 9073 1879 OPEN Monday to Saturday 9am - 5pm

Nettlebed Hospice, Sue Ryder - Oxfordshire

Nettlebed Hospice near Henley-on-Thames offers specialist palliative care to people with life-limiting illnesses from South Oxfordshire, Berkshire and South Buckinghamshire.

Nettlebed Hospice is a Sue Ryder stately care home that is set amidst the birch woodland of Grove Park and can be accessed by the Junction 6 exit of the M40 motorway, running through the heart of Oxfordshire. A sale of donated goods is held every three weeks at the Hospice and on this Saturday morning occasion the forest-lined road outside the main gates to the estate is rammed with cars for a couple of hours. Inside the grounds, parking is provided but the sale is so invariably popular that visitors by car often exceed the designated spaces.

On the approach to the sale area of the grounds, which occupies the outhouses of the hospice building, there is a food stand under a canvas canopy serving hot sandwiches from a rotisserie pig on a spit, conducted by a man in a white butcher's hat and traditional blue and white striped butcher's apron. Visitors with armfuls of junk wander through the grounds and sit on the grassy knolls eating pork baps. There is also a first aid assistant on hand, stationed under a tall isolated pine tree outside the entrance point. All the staff here, identified by an apron and occasional boater hat, are volunteers who give up their Saturdays once a month to run the sale.

The 20p entrance fee is collected on arrival at the stable yard, where the goods that are encountered first are textile based. Trestle tables are set up in the middle of the yard, covered with semi-orderly boxes full of fabrics that range across tablecloths, napkins, handkerchiefs, crochet pieces, swatches and decorative, handmade crafts. Prices are improvised by the women running the stalls, and average out at about 20p for the smaller pieces and 50p to £1 for the larger pieces. In the stables around the yard there are bed linens, furnishing fabrics, duvets, cushions and pillows. My charity shopping companion for today finds a gauzy linen piece – shaped in a cross and embroidered in red cotton thread with the word 'tomato' – which we guess to be a picnic sandwich wrap, and so set about rummaging through the other fabrics to find a 'cucumber', 'salmon' and a much wished-for 'egg'.

Following the signs towards 'Vintage Clothing' I enter another yard selling furniture, including bed frames, doors and electrical goods, with further surrounding outhouses selling vinyl records, children's toys, VHS videos, DVDs and CDs. There is also a room dedicated solely to lampshades. On the path down the hill towards the final goods yard there is a large bookstall under an awning and a prefabricated hut selling an astonishing array of art; original paintings, both amateur and professional, prints and drawings, both framed and unframed, are all very reasonable priced. One large original artwork, skilfully painted and professionally framed, is priced at £50 and when I appear to take a vague interest in its purchase the volunteer who presides over the department invites offers. She tells me that the most valuable donated artworks are sent to Bonham's auction house, but they take a commission on sales and so she explains that she prefers to sell them here where she can, if she knows she can get close to the right price. Bonham's do offer the charity free valuations and a local Henley gallerist also offers his services on a regular basis. 'We've tried every kind of "category management" here but nothing works,' says the volunteer. Nevertheless, there is an orderliness to the stock as the pictures seem to gravitate towards their natural spot in the collection. If it does not sell then the price of a picture is slashed and if it continues not to sell after a few months then it is sent off to one of many regular Sue Ryder shops around the country.

In the final yard there is bric-a-brac, glass and chinaware on tables. One of its outhouses is stuffed with upholstery fabric on rolls. Another room has a huge range of curtains draped over dress rails. Next to this there is a 'jewellery' shed, but the volunteers are now packing up and there is no time to look at any more pieces. Having arrived at the sale at the opening time, it has taken me the full two hours to explore the sale and the imminent closure is announced. Suddenly I become aware of the excitement and tension that has driven me around the site within the strict timeframe; calculated to create the perfect atmosphere to encourage sales.

Trolleys are dotted about the grounds, made from the frame and wheels of an old pram with a plastic crate sitting on top. More robust, purpose-built carts are provided for customers to transport the larger pieces of furniture to their cars. As everyone heads out to leave I meet a woman who tells me that she comes to the sale often, although she does not feel the need to arrive for the opening. 'If I tell myself I have to get here for 10:30am I usually miss it,' she explains, 'but if I take the relaxed attitude and aim to get here whenever I can usually find the time to come.' She has only been here for an hour and she is laden with an unclassified group of objects that will await appropriation of some kind. I come away with a woven rag bag, a Tammy Wynette record, some embroidered linen pieces and a set of dusky pink crocheted rounds that are still hand-tacked to the parchment paper on which they were originally mounted.

ADDRESS Nettlebed Hospice, Nettlebed, Henley-on-Thames, Oxfordshire RG9 5DF OPEN Every third Saturday in the month 10:30am - 12:30pm

Stepping Out - Holloway, London

The Mencap Stepping Out programme offers social and leisure activities during school holidays to teenagers who are affected by profound learning difficulties. A support and information service is also available for parents and carers.

This is an impressive charity shop, preserving the traditional model. It accepts anything and everything and stocks the shop floor with as many donations as possible, from golf clubs and balls, pushchairs, briefcases to a complete range of homeware, with decorative and collectable items. It is a dynamic operation in terms of the sheer volume and range of objects on offer, made accessible by meticulous categorisation and presentation so that the overall impact is not overwhelming. A palimpsest exterior bears the shop's historical fascias since the original Bangs building was first established in 1907. It now faces a shop fittings outlet across the road but nevertheless retains a decrepit interior which suggests that the charity lacks the money to refurbish. Instead, it forges ahead in business with the help of a resourceful team of volunteers.

Four mid-height rails of clothing create corridors up and down the central region of the shop, separated into clothes for women, men and children. They hold a jumbled collection for all seasons that seems not to promise much, although closer inspection identifies several desirable brand names. A Nicole Farhi winter coat is £10 and an Armani summer shirt-dress is £12, both hanging amongst a selection of garments generally more interesting than the usual high street label mainstay.

Around the walls and in front of the windows, bric-a-brac is clustered together in loose collaborations. Every type of utensil and crockery for the kitchen sits in piles at the front alongside a large amount of pressed glassware. Picture frames, ornaments and collectable items are gathered around the shelves by the till. A 1930s pewter tea set, for £125, and a Victorian washing jug and bowl, for £45, are among some of the best pieces. Records are colour coded and priced at either £1.50 or £2.50. In the till counter cabinet, a long glass display case, there are collections of silver cutlery, watches, cameras, jewellery and make-up compacts.

Linen is separated into pillowcases, single and double flat sheets, duvet covers and bedspreads, all pressed and folded. Duvets, quilts and pillows have been steam cleaned and bagged up. On the deep shelves above, there are leather briefcases and children's car seats. Lamp shades are threaded onto a taut line that spans the ceiling, soft toys are strung up together in a hammock and large wooden boxes sit on the floor, filled with frames, prints and paintings.

The back of the shop extends to incorporate another large room for furniture. To the left, a side room is stocked with white goods and miscellaneous consumer electricals, from fridges, washing machines and vacuum cleaners, television sets, video and DVD players to hi-fi systems, microwave ovens, hairdryers and toasters. A 1950s cast-iron Singer sewing machine is £120.

All electricals are PAT tested and come with a three-month guarantee. Amongst the piled corridors of furniture there is a 1930s walnut-veneer and glass cabinet, for £75, and a pristine Victorian Lane oak sideboard, for £345, that I imagine to be the envy of the Holloway Road junk shops and antique furniture dealers nearby. There is functional furniture available here for less money. The shop also sells mattresses and bed frames, doors, tabletops, worktops, ceramic ovens, sofas and armchairs. Wooden and metal-framed chairs hang on a rail around the top of the walls from meat hooks. Two upright pianos, each with beautiful inlay detail, have been freed for playing from the inaccessible stacks of the larger items of furniture.

The overall stock has built up over time from the choice pieces of every small donation, one volunteer explains. As I stand at the counter, she opens a donation carrier bag and is knocked backwards by the smell. Stepping Out is charged by the council to take waste away, which eats into a large proportion of the profits. The charity shop appears to have an enormous advantage over other local businesses with free stock and tax concessions and yet the staff here see its existence on the high street as a continued struggle. 'We are not selling expensive items, but neither is a sweet shop,' the volunteer exclaims. She believes that the key to Stepping Out's survival has been the recent engagement of a van service for collections. Without it the shop would not be able to stock up on the larger, more valuable items of furniture and white goods that are particular bestsellers. Delivery arrangements are made by negotiation and a £5 charge applies.

The volunteer also runs a stall in Brick Lane. She buys in bulk from charity shops and modifies various items to sell on at the market, as a private enterprise. She feels that it is society's collective responsibility to be as resourceful as possible, pointing out that the prices of newly manufactured goods do not adequately reflect the cost of the processes undertaken to produce and distribute them. This makes for unprofitable competition for many small businesses that operate on the principles of reuse. 'Someone suffers at the end of that chain,' she says in regard to bargain consumerism. Her belief is that there are enough manufactured goods in the world not to have to create more and, by redistributing items that would otherwise find their way to landfill sites, the charity shop goes some way towards satiating consumer demand, without exploitation of a labour workforce.

Despite staff confidence in the ethical potential of charity shopping, the assistants are sceptical as to its priority in the public consciousness. People may no longer use the charity shop solely as an opportunity for thrift for themselves but the sourcing of 'original' goods has come to dominate discussions over shoppers' motivations. The volunteers feel that they share with many of their customers an appreciation of the value of the unexpected. It is clear to the volunteer that, 'People enjoy keeping a style or design idea in mind, always looking out for it in the charity shop. Everyone becomes an amateur interior decorator, collector or dealer.' The London theatre and prop houses also buy regularly from the Stepping Out shop.

ADDRESS 128-130 Seven Sisters Road, London N7 7NS TELEPHONE 020 7272 8384 OPEN Monday to Friday 8am - 6pm Saturday 9am - 5pm

Shelter - Stockbridge, Edinburgh

Shelter works to alleviate the distress caused by homelessness and bad housing, by giving advice, information and advocacy to people in housing need and by campaigning for lasting political change to end the housing crisis.

This shop occupies three large units at the end of the commercial stretch of Stockbridge in Edinburgh. The area is characterised by its numerous speciality shops including several charity shops, some of which are among the highest grossing in the UK. Although it sells every kind of commodity, Shelter is known for its clothing, with an emphasis on quality fabrics and predominantly brands that are native to the shops on George Street. The till counter is shrouded in paraphernalia, with neon lights, fake flora and wind chimes giving the appearance of a head shop display, but on closer inspection amidst the decoration the area comprises a selection of curios and the usual knick-knacks, such as picture frames, DVDs, sunglasses, cameras, jewellery, audio books and ornaments.

The shelves throughout the shop are filled with an ever-changing assortment of goods, defined by pockets of particular interest. Children's clothes, games and toys have their own room at the back of the shop. In the adjoining room to the right, there is an entire wall of VHS video tapes whilst a comprehensive collection of menswear and accessories occupies the floor. At the front, a shelving unit of books, with a television set balanced precariously on top and

flickering with a retro grade of image, creates a segregated area for music, which is advertised on the outside by a reflective decoration of CD discs and videos in the correlating front window area.

The consecutive unit is a bookshop that can be accessed only from the street. It is managed separately and subject to different income targets but it is essentially an extension of the same shop, acquired recently from a neighbouring greengrocers. Titles are arranged in alphabetical order along the central shelving unit and by category around the aisle walls. Excess books spill over the front of the shelves and tumbledown towers are poised at the ends, giving the suitably bookish impression that both staff and customers are too absorbed in their subject to put every copy back in order. For those interested in collecting there is an antiquarian section at the back, defined by a large mirror that diffuses orange light over hardback covers from two traditional table lamps amidst the display.

Every year the shop has a January launch for which it saves some of its most valuable items. This year the shop made over £10,000 in the first week and sales have grown by a further ten per cent, constituting currently the biggest charity shop turnover in Scotland. 'This shop has always been a celebration of donations,' says manager Peter Jew, 'competitively but realistically priced.' From time to time the shop gets the top brands. A Vivienne Westwood suit in the window is priced at £100. Anything of notable value is established using reference books and a volunteer team of individuals who are motivated by an interest in clothes. Under Peter's experienced guidance, garments require minimal scrutiny before evaluation. 'Turnover is God here,' Peter continues, 'It's vital we get people interested and keep them coming through the door.'

This is a corporate enterprise but the creative spirit of its staff team is visible throughout the interior styling and the presentation of goods. Peter likens it to the Biba shops of the 1960s, which could be described as the beginning of the 'lifestyle boutique', selling furniture and clothing to self-aware 'creatives' and setting a new marketing model. There is an emphasis on quirky styling and artistic displays here, with lighting playing an important role as well. The aim is to attract young people with disposable incomes and, for those on a budget, to endorse creative decisions over basic provisioning. Biba is responsible for the cliché of Victoriana boutique chic, and the mix and match styling, ornate gold trim decoration and large scale meandering patterns adopted by Peter's team are the decorative elements that have come to represent 'creative living' in the mainstream.

It is evident that Shelter rewards a successful manager with complete creative freedom, to develop their shop's unique character in line with the needs and desires of its local customer base. It takes very seriously its dual charitable purpose, as a local service as well as its fundraising responsibility to its cause, maintaining that this duality is at the very heart of its business structure. 'If you're not pleasing the customers – if you don't put them first – then you won't get the patronage to make the money for the charity,' adds Peter. This shop relies entirely on doorstep donations.

There is a strict policy in place that ensures nothing is made available from behind the scenes to dealers or collectors, and staff are only entitled to purchase an item officially once it has been out on the floor for a minimum

of twenty-four hours. A discount of one third off clothing is offered and the rest of the goods are charged at the full price, to demonstrate that there are few privileges given to anyone over the public.

Attracted to the possibility of working in a vibrant atmosphere, staff are engaged in innovative styling projects and given the opportunity to learn about retail and successful business structures. In return, the shop gratefully maintains almost full volunteer cover, which includes several Duke of Edinburgh volunteers under the age of twenty and one woman, certainly over the age of eighty, who has worked at the shop since it opened and accepted all the changes that have been made over the years. The core volunteer workforce is in their fifties.

When I visit in September the shop is already selling Christmas cards. It makes a lot of money from charity cards, particularly at Christmas, and so it must work with the demand. 'Customers expect the same seasonal provisions as the main high street shops and so we have to take advantage of that where we can,' Peter explains. The front window is used to theme the shop, attract new interest and to showcase prime merchandise. Today the window is full of designer carrier bags to promote the shop's aim to stop buying carrier bags and to encourage the public to donate their old carrier bags for reuse. Shelter works with a company called Precycle to take away items that are edited out of the donations, for recycling.

ADDRESS 104-106 Raeburn Place, Stockbridge, Edinburgh EH4 1HH TELEPHONE 0131 343 2963 OPEN Monday to Saturday 9:30am - 6pm, Sunday 12pm - 5pm

Shakespeare's Hospice Recycling Shop - Stratford

Shakespeare's Hospice offers specialist palliative nursing care and support to enable local patients to continue living at home with their families while receiving active treatment.

Coming out of Books Etcetera, the Shakespeare's Hospice's specialist bookshop in Stratford town centre (see 'Books'), I happened to ask directions from a man who in fact lived next door to the Hospice Recycling Centre and had 'just bought a Chuck Berry CD from there.' I drove out of Stratford, past Ann Hathaway's cottage, towards Warwick on the A46. I arrived within twenty minutes at Burton Farm in Bishopton where, next to Warwickshire County Council Tip, the Shakespeare's Hospice Recycling Shop can be found. I drive past the 'Barn Studios' and hand-written sign advertising 'free range eggs', at the entrance, and on to the Tip site.

The Recycling Centre is a light industrial warehouse that cuts in on the road leading up to the Tip, in order to intercept drivers and give staff the opportunity to check a car boot full of items destined for the scrapheap, picking out the things they know they can sell on behalf of the Hospice. Tip-site shops are such an excellent, simple and resourceful idea that they are becoming more common. The shops directly help to reduce landfill at the point of disposal and the impact of this is clearly visible here. This shop, immediately evident on approach to the tip, is particularly well-stocked, selling absolutely every type of junk that has been ordered, categorised and loaded on to a maze of shelving that divides up the vast corrugated iron unit. Despite its unconventional face, I am told by one long-standing member of staff that the shop provides the Hospice with a turnover of about £200,000 per year, making it the charity's most successful outlet.

Most of the staff here are young men – community service workers – dressed in a uniform of neon orange jackets, who sift through and group the goods as they come in. When I take pictures of the site I am not allowed to photograph anyone wearing one of these jackets. Trevor is one of three paid staff at the shop. He was an electrician for the Health Service for over twenty-five years before he lost his wife a couple of years ago and decided to take early retirement. He quickly became restless and came to work at the Recycling Centre three days a week. This year, however, he turns sixty-five and is required to retire once and for all, although he does not want to, he tells me, because the Centre has done much to help him through a difficult time. He found his current partner through working here. He was playing a Dean Martin CD and a woman approached him to ask him to identify the music. He sold her the CD for £1 and now they are moving in together, once they find a place of their own. He points to a microwave: 'I needed a compact one for our new place and this one just came in. A staff perk,' he says, as he puts it aside for his own purchase. Trevor goes on to point out how both instances serve to illustrate the unpredictability of life, 'You never know what's around the corner.' For me, this also highlights the particular appeal of the charity shop. 'We try to hang on to the weird and wonderful because you just never know what is going to turn up in those black bags!' one volunteer adds.

There are no price tags attached to the items and instead a senior staff member offers prices on the spot, on request. 'That surely leaves you open to bartering,' I suggest. 'That's all part of it,' he replies, recognising how much people enjoy and thrive on this kind of shopping experience. He tells me that he is 'a good judge of a customer's wallet'. He then does the 'hard sell' on me: Royal Family memorabilia is collected together in several plastic buckets on an outside table and I pick out a 'Charles and Di' mug. 'Collectable!' he says instantly. 'I'd usually say £3 but I'll do it for you for £2.'

It states on a series of signs outside that the Centre cannot sell large or bulky items due to a lack of space but every type of manufactured object and machine seems to be represented here in some quantity, from a motorised eggcup to a three-piece suite. There is even compost for the garden. Bicycles range from £15 to £75, all reconditioned beautifully by a scheme run by the local prison. Electrical equipment is reconditioned to fully working order and tested for safety. Trevor himself refurbishes anything that comes in, if he has space for it. Kenwood mixers with ceramic bowls are about £35 and, he clicks his fingers, '...will sell like that.' Dyson vacuum cleaners are £25. TVs only sell with their remote controls – because so many sets come in, the shop does not need to sell the ones without.

People who shop here obviously expect a high standard of goods. 'Otherwise they'd go and buy it for cheap from the big supermarkets,' Trevor points out. He knows his market and the competition that the Hospice is up against in the form of multinational supermarket chains. The challenge is to attract customers away from the budget retail companies. As I leave a customer makes an offer on a collection of goods, 'A pound for this lot?' she asks, looking down at an armful of books and a flowerpot, and he accepts. The relaxed and experienced approach from the staff here is refreshing and reassuring, and the policy clearly works well for the Hospice.

ADDRESS Burton Farm, Bishopton; on the A46 outside Stratford-Upon-Avon TELEPHONE 01789 299 285 OPEN Monday to Sunday 9am - 3:30pm.

Earl Mountbatten Hospice Department Store - Newport, Isle Of Wight

EMH cares for the islanders facing life-limiting conditions to give them the best quality of life possible with dignity and love. The charity believes in a holistic approach including medical, complementary and spiritual care.

This is an award-winning shop, based on profits made for the parent charity. It has, over the years, continued to expand and now occupies a row of retail units along the street. Unlike the familiar nationals it has chosen to expand within a quieter area of the town and retains a shabby charm, in line with the character of the Isle of Wight but not often found in its more ambitious fundraising competitors. The merchandise is well considered, as is the aesthetic of the store, and includes only sellable goods at realistic prices. To add a personal touch, price tags on every item are handwritten. The clothes are steam-cleaned and immaculately presented.

The shop describes itself as a 'department store' to reflect the comprehensive selection of goods in every 'department' familiar to the charity shop. Each section is stocked with quality merchandise that is presented carefully. On entering the shop the customer is faced with a wide selection of women's clothing. Plus sizes are well catered for, exclusively occupying one long rail.

Select items of furniture are used to segregate the shop floor as well as providing a diversity of goods. Full sets of crockery are set up on tabletops to suggest an elaborate dining experience and around the floor there are plenty of paintings, stacked up against the table legs and the skirts of the rails. Original artworks range from £15 to £45.

In the next unit, there is a large collection of kitchenware, crockery and glassware. At the back is a children's section, big enough to contain more than an average charity shop's overall stock. In addition to the homeware on sale there are toys, games, ornaments and a few curios, spread across both regions of the room. A giant dolls' house sits together with a selection of dog muzzles and an electronic manicure kit.

The next room along is taken up with menswear for every occasion and is a thoroughfare to the final enclave of retro clothing, advertised creatively by a sign pinned to a white wedding dress. Displays on the shelves contain antique dial telephones as props, all for sale at good prices. In another area, linens and furnishings are grouped together, beautifully maintained despite customers' foraging fingertips. I buy an Aquascutum silk shirt for £5 and a hand-embroidered handkerchief for £1.50.

Like many charity shops which can be regarded as an easy target, EMH in Newport is a frequent victim of theft. The shop feels vulnerable in more ways than one to those prepared to undermine its fundraising ambitions. Retail manager Julie Clifton feels that she must be continuously vigilant about undervalued stock bought for the purpose of selling on at a profit, on eBay or at one of the island's many car-boot sales. 'Charity shops have to protect themselves,' she asserts. This shop tries to minimise theft by keeping the more valuable stock behind the staffed till counter and installing conspicuous security cameras, but it also holds back from the shop floor altogether the most desirable donations. These are reserved for auction. Many charity shops have now set up an auction site online, but administering this is time consuming and requires an adept taskforce.

EMH does not lack volunteers to run its operation and so each section is staffed. A large proportion of the island's residents are over retirement age and this is commonly the most forthcoming volunteer group. 'Unless you can afford to pay them you can't get the young people to work in the charity shops. They like to come in and buy things but they don't give anything back. They haven't got the time to spare,' remarks Julie. Relying predominantly on volunteers means that the shop lacks a highly-trained retail workforce. Julie gives an anecdotal example of a customer who holds up a synthetic velvet dress and asks a volunteer, 'Can you tell me what this fabric is?' The simple answer is 'velvet'. 'Yes, but is it cotton or nylon?' the customer prompts. 'It's velvet!' is the closing reply, from a volunteer who doesn't know there is more than one type. Julie comments, 'Unless you've got an expert, you can't be sure that you're not losing a lot of money.'

This highlights for me the battle charity shops have with the perceived 'actual value' of goods determined by the international marketplace online and the value achievable within a local scope. Their primary pledge of responsibility to fundraising for their cause inevitably comes into conflict with customers' interests. Sustaining a relationship with the donating public

178

relies on acknowledging and accommodating this anomaly. A conscious return to a more indiscriminate pricing system could be regarded as accepting the limitations of such a business. The alternative appears to be a move away from a local customer base and towards the world wide web.

ADDRESS 19-23 Lugley Street, Newport, Isle of Wight PO30 5HD
TELEPHONE 01983 825 647 OPEN Monday to Friday 9:30am - 4:30pm, Saturday 9:30am - 4pm

Katharine House Hospice Recycling Centre has been open since December 2007 and is already making money for the hospice. The premises are conveniently located on St Albans Road in Stafford, just up the road from the tip, and it invites the public to call in to see if there is anything of which it could make use before it becomes waste that goes to landfill. The warehouse recycles a variety of household waste to raise money for the hospice. It accepts metals such as brass, aluminium and copper. Other items such as mobile phones and compact discs can also be utilised. ADDRESS St Alban's Road Industrial Estate, Stafford, Staffordshire ST16 3DR TELEPHONE 01785 254645 OPEN Monday to Friday 9:30am - 4:30pm, Saturday and Sunday 10am - 2pm

Furniture at the Salvation Army, Kelvinhall in Glasgow. This is a Salvation Army Trading Company Limited shop (SATCoL) within one of the three Scottish divisions of the SA. There are at least sixteen different charity shops along this road and the SA is the largest, offering the greatest range of goods. It operates a two-day returns policy on all items. ADDRESS 91 Dumbarton Road, Glasgow G11 6PW TELEPHONE 0141 334 7253 OPEN Monday to Saturday 9am - 5.30pm

In a trial collection scheme for Kirkwood Hospice, Huddersfield, unwanted gifts, toys, books and clothing were packed into special 'blue bags' and collected by hospice volunteer drivers. After a good response, approximately fifty bags were picked up and delivered to the hospice shop on Byram Street, Huddersfield. The shop recently dressed its mannequins with the blue bags as a statement to promote the shop's move to go carrier bag free. ADDRESS 5 Byram Street, Huddersfield, West Yorkshire HD1 1BX TELEPHONE 01484 430 326 OPEN Monday to Friday 9am - 5pm

The International Aid Trust furniture warehouse in Tarleton sells miscellaneous second-hand goods, from consumer electrical appliances to large-scale household furniture suites. ADDRESS Longton Business Park, Station Road, Much Hoole, Preston PR4 5LE TELEPHONE 01772 611 122 OPEN Monday to Friday 9am - 4:30pm, Saturday 11am - 4pm

The Community Shop, Leeds sells clothing, toys and household goods as well as records, books and furniture in the unit next door. ADDRESS 14-16 Gren Road, Meanwood, Leeds LS6 6AJ TELEPHONE 0113 275 3533 OPEN Monday to Saturday 10am - 4pm

YMCA, Hove (see page 162).

Mannequins and the domes at Guild Care, East Worthing (see page 164).

Oxfam - Ilkley, West Yorkshire

Oxfam provides tools to enable people to become self-supporting and opens markets of international trade where crafts and produce from poorer regions of the world can be sold at a fair price to benefit the producer.

Along the Victorian streets of Ilkley, in bloom with floral displays during my visit, I predictably encounter an Oxfam shop – an unmodernised branch, a few doors down from Betty's Café Tea Rooms. Streams of tourists walk by without paying too much attention, surprisingly, to the attractive window display of vintage tablecloths and crocheted and embroidered linens. Ilkley is a wealthy dormitory town of nearby cities Leeds and Bradford. The company Woolmark is an employer here but the town relies mostly on tourism.

Inside this Oxfam is busy and appears to be thriving for the most part on local custom. Addressing this demand, manager Paul Felgate caters for local events with themed collections from week to week. The annual local grammar school 'ball' inspires an 'Eveningwear' week, leading up to the event. In preparation, all decent evening outfits are sent to the shop from the other local Oxfams. A link is maintained between the regional shops, which together mastermind local promotional events, rotating stock between them.

Paul feels he has practical autonomy from charity headquarters in the way that he chooses to run the shop, which revises my pre-conceptions that Oxfam shops are managed by the executives on a tight rein and stocked from a rationalised hub. In fact, the centralised systems that are put in place by Oxfam are an invaluable resource for the local level of shop. The Oxfam Wastesaver Centre is located conveniently in nearby Huddersfield, which processes a massive twelve thousand tonnes of clothes, textiles and shoes that cannot be handled through the shops, for recycling, export or resale. Donated items stay on the shop floor for about two weeks before they are sent there.

The shop is often given cashmere jumpers, for example, but Paul finds he cannot sell them in any kind of damaged state. They go straight to Wastesaver because each garment, stained, ripped, or perished, achieves around £7, for shredding and reuse of the cashmere fibre. Everything sent to the depot is either re-graded or ragged. If re-graded, it is sent to Developing Countries or to those with immediate aid needs, 'So everything gets a second chance,' Paul says.

As is indicated by the stock displayed in the front window, the current promotional theme at the Ilkley branch is 'Linen'. The shop has saved up its most prized donations of this kind and is selling an impressive selection of vintage examples of quality textiles and craft techniques. 'We do much better when we save up the good stuff and then put it out all together as a big promotion, with a themed window display,' Paul explains. 'At the moment we are taking between £70 and £90 a day, just on linen.' All the white linen has all been carefully starched and ironed. A Victorian cotton raglan top with hand-crocheted square yolk is £14.99, faintly damaged. The condition of the pieces is described on their labels. No detail, whether it is a positive attribute or not, has been overlooked. There are immaculate sets of cross-stitched napkins and individually embellished handkerchiefs. The tablecloths hanging in the window are some of the finest specimens in this collection, priced at £50 a piece. An alternative craft book, *Making Stuff*, is available at the end of the large island display unit.

The shop has about seventy expert volunteers working to value and advise on merchandise. Music, books and furnishings are a rudimentary cross-section of interests, as well as linen. There are ten volunteers that specialise in books alone and this is reflected in the large and comprehensive book section at the back of the shop, with subsections on every popular topic. There is an exceptionally good range of home furnishings, with four full rails occupying two walls. During my visit a woman comes in to the shop asking the volunteer if she would take a donation of 'knitted squares', because her elderly mother-in-law occupies herself with knitting them. Paul gives her some of the simple knitting patterns they have in the shop to take away with her. In the corner, a 4p photocopier provides a further practical facility for the local clientele, cementing its image as a faithful community shop.

ADDRESS 40 Grove Road, Ilkley Yorkshire LS29 9QF TELEPHONE 01943 602 524 OPEN Monday to Saturday 9am - 5pm, Sunday 1pm - 4pm

St. Columba's Hospice
- Leith, Edinburgh

Committed to the highest standards of care for patients with active, progressive, far-advanced illnesses and support for their relatives and carers.

The St. Columba's Hospice Shops Limited runs an independent group of five shops, dedicated to raising funds for St Columba's Hospice. Previously known as The Doo'cot (Dovecot), this particular branch occupies a double-fronted retail space in a tenement building near the top of Leith Walk. It is exceptional in every department, in its presentation, selection and quality of merchandise and in terms of its generous volunteer staff. It is difficult therefore to confine it to any one section of this book, but as it is renowned for its linen goods I include it in the 'Furnishings & Linen' section.

The Leith shop is highly traditional in many ways although its approach to business feels more modern than most of its contemporaries. There is a willingness here to adapt traditional values to meet the needs of its gentrified locale and it follows the contemporary fashion of revisiting traditional craft pastimes such as needlework, knitting and sewing. An elegant interior showcases clothing, ceramics and collectables as well as superb linens, furnishings and home-crafts sections, each scattered with practical tools and beautiful pieces for the home. Tongue-and-groove wood panels clad the walls in sage green and the worn polish on an oak board floor underfoot further enriches the backdrop.

Recently refurbished, the shop has maintained its identity and charm, simply re-jigging the layout in order to use the space better. The till counter has moved to a position facing the entrance door, making more room for the clothing section to the right. All the clothes, for both men and women, are steamed and hung on portable rails around the front portion of the shop, behind the deep window display area, curtained off with tartan drapery. Along the distance of almost the entire depth of the unit on the left side there runs a series of wide-set shelves, full of bric-a-brac. Amongst the ephemera common to any charity shop there is a lot of desirable and collectable china here. A hand-painted bone china tea set is £10. Large serving plates are priced at £2.50. Baskets lined with ticking cloth, made by the volunteers, gather every last piece of useful cast-offs, for 50p. Classical records are 50p each or three for £1. There is a good selection of vinyl singles. An antique display cabinet contains a range of jewellery. Books are half price, including an almost complete series of Mills and Boon novels. *Mojo* magazines dating back to the 90s are also 50p. A tremendous amount of care has gone into their presentation.

Continuing up a small set of open stairs to a mezzanine level, the shelving becomes part of a dedicated linen area. There is plenty of bedding, such as hand-knitted wool blankets for around £4 and patchwork quilts. Kitchen linen includes tea towels and tablecloths, many of which are well-preserved vintage examples. There is a basket of new, crisp white percale cotton sheets and duvet covers as well as a container of material scraps of all sizes. Buttons are collected individually and collectively on cards. Lined curtains start at £10 and when I mention to the staff a particular preference one volunteer brings up from the stockroom several examples that fit the description. There are needles for knitting, embroidery and lace-making along with vintage needlework and dressmaking patterns. Instruction books and half-finished pieces of embroidery offer beginners an entry point to the craft. The shop used to allow the public access to an upstairs linen stockroom, on special occasions, and to students in particular, until health and safety regulations made this untenable.

St Columba's Hospice shop is staffed by a group of committed and loyal volunteers and a paid manager. I meet one volunteer, now in her nineties, who has worked at the Leith shop for over seventeen years (the shop has been open for eighteen years) and has been associated with the Hospice for over twenty years. She is in charge of pricing the ceramic goods as they come in. Another elderly volunteer evaluates the linens. Both women comment on the lasting friendships they have made whilst working over the years in the shop.

Manager Margaret McAlpine and the staff have a disarmingly generous attitude to the customers, prioritising in all their comments the importance of the donating public to the enterprise. They discuss the pricing policy from this angle. 'People expect low prices in a charity shop and we want to give them high quality goods at prices they can afford,' Margaret says. There is a sense of duty to the donors and a shared obligation to put an appropriate price on items. The charity strongly believes that in this way the shop can give something back to its patrons. At the same time, the price attached to an item must reflect as closely as possible its standard market value, out of a respect for their donor and to encourage customers to continue to part with more lucrative items, secure in the knowledge that their value will be appreciated. 'We can't be seen just to slap any old price on to an object. If customers saw that they'd be reluctant to give us their nicer stuff. It is our responsibility to get the best price for an item on behalf of each benefactor,' adds one volunteer. The staff continue to discuss posting 'thank you' notices for individual donations in the local newspaper.

This tallies with the original dual concept of the charity shop, to help a needy section of the community with affordable clothing and homeware whilst raising money for the local hospice. Located just beyond the Pilrig Church boundary, Leith is a traditionally working class area of Edinburgh. Where the charity shop has long recognised its own unique and invaluable encouragement of public recycling whilst also providing an outlet for charitable giving, the Leith shop in particular seems to prioritise a high regard for its customers in order to sustain this business model.

St. Columba's also runs a Trading Company in Morningside, specialising in books and gifts (see 'Books, Music and Film').

ADDRESS 352 Leith Walk, Edinburgh EH6 5BR TELEPHONE 0131 555 1526 OPEN Monday to Saturday 10am - 4pm

St. Luke's - Tavistock, Devon

St Luke's Hospice Plymouth provides care to hundreds of people a year from throughout the South West of Devon and the South East of Cornwall, incorporating practical, financial, and emotional support.

This St Luke's Hospice shop is the second of two Tavistock branches incorporated into the town's distinctive stone terraces, alongside the historic Pannier Market buildings on Duke Street. It concentrates on linens, for which it has gained an international reputation through the online marketplace. It displays it wares in its two front windows to the local community and passing tourists, clearly distinguishing itself as a specialist shop and using the pieces on display to demonstrate how to use antique textiles within the home. Here they create a period backdrop for the layering of bric-a-brac in front, draping the fabric to divide and create space, partitioning off the window scenes from the interior of the shop.

Inside, the shop is small and crammed to capacity with selections of clothing and bric-a-brac. The focus across the back wall is the tightly packed rails of white table and bed linen, all washed, starched and pressed for immaculate presentation. Daylight filters into the room through net curtains, evoking the controlled lighting conditions of a museum or the private chambers of an historic residence.

Some of the best examples of skilled embroidery are unfurled and tacked to the wall behind the till counter. Matching sets of tablecloths and napkins are generally priced between £20 and £30. All the pieces are tagged and offer explanations on the type and quality of the textiles and handiwork. Many of the items are labelled 'vintage' but still do not demand a great deal more in price. Where the items are marked or damaged they are noted as 'imperfect'.

The antiques are imbued with a rich sense of history and the tradition of 'waste not, want not', from the time when many of these fabrics were produced, resonates strikingly with the current principles of charity shopping. Textiles were readily repaired, remade and re-fashioned for continued reuse. Clothing was modified or remade to accommodate the latest fashions, or passed on as 'hand-me-downs' to another person. Worn sheets, clothing and tablecloths were customarily cut down to become napkins, pillowcases or towels. Smaller sections became quilt squares, patches and cleaning rags. En masse these crafted pieces become a beautiful monument of resourcefulness.

The collection of linen here is extensive, considering the restrictions on space. The age of the second-hand pieces, spanning in many cases more than a generation, testifies to their quality, the likes of which would be far less affordable in new goods. One customer, clearly passionate about the textiles and a regular patron of the shop, tells me, 'Fabrics made in the old days used pure fibres, made without harsh chemicals like chlorine bleach. Any chemical processes that were used in production would have dissipated by now. People with allergies like them.'

There are soft and starched linens of various weights available. Hem-stitched Irish Linen damasks, Jacobean embroidery and tatting techniques are all highlighted. There is a range of simple, traditional and more whimsical designs. Classic emblems such as wreaths and ribbons and embroidered scallops are popular, and there are many monogrammed handkerchiefs. Wedding handkerchiefs are commonly edged with needle-point lace. The smaller collections and odd pieces such as Maltese lace rounds, coasters, collars and cuffs are piled up neatly in plastic baskets under the rail.

Tavistock has a sizeable and rapidly growing community and there are several linen shops in the town that cater to a clearly popular demand for crafted textiles and haberdashery. The Panniers Market has a Linen Press stall, Linens & Things is a furnishings cooperative shop and there is a home textiles area and haberdashers in the small department store in the town. Such an abundance of crafted textiles means that this charity shop is never short of donations, nor of expert volunteers to manage the second-hand stock. The volunteer at the till appears confident in her subject and readily offers advice on how to appropriately use of textiles in the home. When I inspect a figurative jacquard 'show' towel, she suggests that it would make a good runner for the table.

In a modern context, many of these fabrics require a 'lifestyle' application, dressing the home for show. More practical goods such as bath towels are neatly folded in plastic storage boxes underneath the clothing rails on one side, along with pairs of lined curtains in bags and a limited amount of bed sheets, pillowcases and bedspreads, most of which is made of cheap polycotton. After pawing the antiques, the examples of modern manufacturing are off-putting but lead me to take note, nevertheless, that all interests and needs are catered for here, in textile form.

ADDRESS 14 Duke Street, Tavistock, PL19 0BA TELEPHONE 01822 617 777
OPEN Monday to Saturday 9am - 4:30pm

Linenbox, Heart Of Kent Hospice - Lenham, Kent

The Hospice provides in-patient care for up to twelve people at any one time. The Community Team provides much needed support and advice to patients in their homes, whilst others benefit from the Day Therapy service.

This outlet, now in its ninth year as a charity shop, is housed in a 13th century building in the historic village of Lenham. There is a large proportion of elderly people in the village and the volunteer I speak to remembers having her hair washed as a little girl in the back room of the shop, now the Linenbox, when it was a ladies' hairdressers. The building has typically small doors and low ceilings, with a traditional wooden beam construction visible between the thick insulated walls, within which a restful silence settles on its contents. These romantic surroundings have a long, rich history that has brought with it the deposits of merchandise on sale here.

The front room of the shop has rails of clothing for both men and women, butted together on a perpendicular angle to fill the small space. There are shelving units around the perimeter of the room, presenting small selections of books, bric-a-brac, crockery, toys and games, as well as more collectable items in the till counter cabinet. A selection of homemade jams is available, as it is throughout all the Heart of Kent hospice shops, made by a local cottage industry. Handbags and shoes are brand new. Many of the donations to the Lenham branch are passed on to the charity's main shop in Aylesford, where there is paid staff and more space for a larger range of stock. Most books go to the shops with dedicated book sections, in West Malling and Maidstone.

The Corner House shop does particularly good business in quality linen and soft furnishings, which is contained exclusively in the back room that is signposted above the doorway with a needlepoint piece. A Turkish wool pile rug on the floor and choice pieces of home furniture make a homely and elegant context for the merchandise. A window seat bench is stacked wall-to-wall with cushions. Curtain ties hang from hooks by the door and the stack of discretely patterned lampshades piled on top of each other is reminiscent of a totem pole. Framed prints are displayed close to the floor on easel stands and ornate picture frames are propped on top of small side tables in the corners of the room. There is a good selection of hats and a long rail of lined curtains. Facing the rails there is a reproduction period dresser laden with neatly pressed and labelled piles of bed linen.

The shop and its contents seem deeply significant in light of its main customer base, most of whom are in the later stages of life. Workbaskets with half finished tapestries and handmade clothes are treasured remnants of peoples' lives, imbued with the memories of their previous owners. 'People die but their possessions do not,' says one elderly volunteer. 'A lot of these items have been precious to someone and they bring with them a great sentiment'. She speculates over a series of cake plates as to how many birthday cakes have been served on them. I continue to scour through the items with a heightened awareness of the social life of things. All the goods I see and covet have been seen and coveted by someone else. Despite the atmosphere here, the items are stripped of their original meaning, left merely the spectres of their past lives. All must be re-commodified according to their material value and so they wait here, temporarily removed from circulation, for someone to re-appropriate their use. Handling these artefacts triggers the imagination, sharpens a sense of empathy for the human relationship to objects and celebrates the continuity of life.

ADDRESS Shop B, The Corner House, Faversham Road, Lenham ME17 8QDF TELEPHONE 01622 851 618 OPEN Monday to Friday 10am - 4pm Saturday 10am - 1pm

Martlets, Hove has a good stock of new wool and a room at the back of the shop dedicated to linen and furnishings. ADDRESS 97 Blatchington Road, Hove BN3 3YG TELEPHONE 01273 747 297 OPEN Monday - Saturday 9:30am - 4:30pm

Handkerchiefs at St Luke's (see page 192).

Shop window at Kirkwood Hospice, Honley ADDRESS 21 Westgate, Honley,
West Yorkshie HD9 6AA TELEPHONE 01484 661503 OPEN Monday to Saturday
9am - 5pm

Brightly coloured linen at St. Leonards Hospice, York ADDRESS Acomb
Regent Buildings, York Road, Acomb, York YO26 4LT TELEPHONE 01904 788
063 OPEN Monday to Saturday 9am - 4pm

MI0004688655

ISBN-0-8283-1425-x

FURNITURE » » »

St. Luke's Interiors - Winsford, Cheshire

St Luke's Cheshire Hospice is a small hospice situated in Winsford that cares for people living in the mid and south Cheshire area.

There is another St. Luke's Cheshire shop in Dingle Walk in Winsford but the Delemere Street branch brokers upmarket furniture and collectable homeware. 'Interiors' opened in 2006 to meet popular demand for traditional and antique goods for the home, by putting to use the valuable commodities generated from house clearances in the area. This is a rural region with a high concentration of villages. Winsford was given 'New Town' status in the 1970s but it is a conurbation with a long and varied history and considerable wealth, from industry as well as tourism.

'Customers come from far and wide to visit and the general consensus is that we have an attractive and welcoming shop that looks more like a Habitat than a charity shop,' says co-manager Carol. Many people visiting for the first time do not even realise that the merchandise on sale is donated to help raise money for the local Hospice. To raise awareness for the cause, flyers are placed about the shop that identify it as a charity shop and reveal the fundraising needs of the hospice which currently costs £5,200 per day to run. The care home is located ten minutes away by car and local customers tend to be familiar with the charity, which helps to give them a sense of patronage when shopping here. Supporters make a special visit to Interiors because it stocks items that the other hospice shops cannot, due to the size of premises, insurance restrictions or because other branches are unable to showcase certain items in the most advantageous light.

Furniture is sent to this shop, within the St. Luke's retail group in order to achieve the highest prices. With the assistance of the Area Manager, St. Luke's staff keep up with the prices and changing fashions at local auctions, and also buy bric-a-brac items to supplement stock and dress the shop. Dark wood, I am told, has not been popular at auction recently and the collection in the shop is therefore blonde in tone. The Interiors layout includes a series of tableaux that reflect the lifestyles portrayed in interiors magazines, making it easier for customers to picture an item of furniture in their own home, to understand its value and to accept its higher than average charity shop price. A sale on selected items runs every six to eight weeks, to make way for new merchandise. The shop has started to pay a driver to collect and deliver furniture.

Many of the pieces on sale are suggestive of the bureaucratic classes of the area's industrial past. There is a writing bureau and filing drawers from the turn of the century. The volunteers believe that a long-standing craft tradition has brought with it an innate Winsfordian sensitivity to quality craftsmanship and items that carry a local history, such as earthenware and salt-glazed stoneware, remain particularly popular. I buy two traditional wood blocks cut in a floral design to use as a repeat pattern for textile printing. They have been used but they are in immaculate condition and priced at a premium £10 each. There is a reasonably large selection of collectable Potteries china, including tea sets, vases, dinner services, along with traditional boxed cutlery sets, polished and presented selectively.

All upholstered furniture in St. Luke's carries a fire retardant label. The shop does not sell beds or electricals. It focuses mainly on smaller items, such as sets of drawers, of which it currently stocks an attractive Edwardian example, side tables, chairs, sofas and suites, including those for the garden. Much of the furniture is antique or reproductions of traditional designs to suit the rural context. A robust, solid oak farmhouse table and ten chairs is £1,500. Sofas are around £300. Chairs are especially popular to furnish the home and place its style within a particular period. Captain's chairs arrive frequently and sell for around £100. One elegant Georgian chair with square proportions and clean dovetail joints is priced at £175.

There is a small room at the back of the shop that houses a rail of furnishings – mainly curtains – and customers are asked to seek help from a member of staff to browse the collection. The shop has just sold a pair of jacquard cotton curtains for £75, but the average price is around £20 for a fully lined pair.

The shop has an ongoing relationship with a London-based artist who customises traditional furniture to create unique pieces of interest for the shop. A large leather trunk is painted with a rural scene and a magazine rack is decorated with a decoupage technique. Local artists also offer their work for sale through the shop on a commission basis and there are several oil and watercolour paintings hanging around the walls. These work well as a backdrop for the furniture but the staff limit the sale of such stock, which requires a lot of paperwork.

Each volunteer has found a particular area of interest on which to focus and they are quickly becoming experts in their field, creating a professional body in interior design. One woman describes her route into the job, from a position as the Head of Laundry and then Head Chef at the Hospice before leaving to have a baby. On returning to work, this time cleaning, she heard that the Interiors shop required part-time help. She took up a role here as a way to rebuild her confidence and experience after maternity leave, exemplifying another type of charity shop volunteer besides the commonly identified groups of retired and unemployed citizens.

Run entirely by women, Interiors reflects the majority of its customer base and anticipates successfully the tastes and needs of its female clientele. Cheshire is home to many earning high salaries and there is a consistently low rate of unemployment. Traditional family values are prevalent with a high proportion of women in the role of homemaker.

ADDRESS 70 Delamere Street, Winsford, Cheshire CW7 2LU TELEPHONE 01606 590 006 OPEN Monday to Saturday 9:30am - 5pm

The Maxie Richards Foundation
- Partick, Glasgow

The Maxie Richards Foundation is a Christian charity
supporting Kings Court residential home and numerous
practical and rehabilitative projects for recovering addicts.

This shop is one of three, exclusive to Glasgow, run professionally by The
Maxie Richards Foundation. It is an exemplary model of the charity's aims,
to sell donated furniture to the public to raise funds and also to integrate the
direct recipients of the charity into the running of the retail organisation by
employing them. The shop is situated on the commercial stretch of a low-
income area of Glasgow, packed with local charity shops, many of which also
have the space to sell furniture. From the outside this shop is as unassuming
as the others but inside it is stocked with goods of outstanding quality and
style.

The corner retail unit is large and square, with black and white
checkerboard tiles on the floor and mirrored mosaic tiles decorating the
ceiling columns. It is occupied by items of furniture that are impressive in
their grand proportions, suggesting that their origins lie in wealthy homes.
The quality of the stock demands a high price that seems inconsistent with
the catchment area. Nevertheless, at the entrance, a carved oak four-poster
bed commands a justifiable £400 and the price of a Steinway grand piano is
yet to be decided. I look keenly at a Hilton & Hilton upright piano, sofas and
suites, dressing tables, writing bureaux and a simple museum cabinet that
is not for sale but instead provides the showcase for an elegant selection of
china. A chest of drawers in the window is accompanied by a cutting from a
style magazine exhibiting a similar piece.

There are several neighbouring house-clearance companies along the street
and, to ensure they remain ahead of the competition, the charity's dedicated
driver works hard to coordinate a delivery and collection service that runs
five days a week, with the assistance of 'Start Up' and Community Service
volunteers. Being a drug-related charity the Foundation is low on the public-
donations list and so it must also rely in part on a source of supply direct from
private companies. Its 'scratch and dent' goods – imperfect furniture, unfit
for new sale in the shops – sell very well as second-hand stock in the charity
shops.

The Foundation runs a 20,000 square foot factory in Port Glasgow that
provides the space for the various skilled manual jobs required to support
this charitable venture. All furniture can be renovated here and there is a
constant need for the repair of suites, wardrobes and tables. An upholstery
department oversees the re-covering of seats and chairs. There is a 'sanding'
section where large pieces, such as tables, drawers and wardrobes, can be
revitalised, whilst the antique department looks after the furniture requiring
more tender care.

The charity's individual recipients – the residents of Kings Court – are engaged to work here, trained by upholsterer John McCormack, a grade one tradesman who had his own upholstery business in Inverness for eighteen years. A master woodcarver comes regularly to the factory to teach woodcarving skills to the apprentices. The Glasgow economy is traditionally dominated by shipbuilding and the charity has taken on a major three year restoration project, dedicated to renovating the 'cockle bawley' ship The Resolute, used in the Second World War to rescue British expeditionary forces. The symbolism of this history is not lost on the religious minds of the charity organisers.

Using skills developed at the factory the plan is for the charity to manufacture a significant proportion of the shops' goods itself. Easels, small carved jewellery boxes and canvas frames are three products the team are considering focusing on. 'By using old, antique wood we intend to make small boxes which our lads will carve designs on. This will give the boxes a good selling point,' says Pat.

This is a social enterprise born out of a conscious religious impulse, reaching beyond the usual scope of a charity shop. By integrating the very people the charity is set up to help, it not only provides a focus to assist their rehabilitation but it also offers them a direct and motivating interest in fundraising. Recognising that the Foundation can tap into a growing market for goods with an enterprising and ethical provenance, the factory hopes to open a showroom to the public sometime soon.

ADDRESS 550 Dumbarton Road, Glasgow G11 6RH TELEPHONE 0141 334 779 OPEN Monday to Saturday 9:30am - 3:30pm

Low-cost wares are advertised on eye-catching yellow posters at the British Heart Foundation, Bradford. ADDRESS 50-54 Westgate, Bradford, West Yorkshire BD1 2QR TELEPHONE 01274 722 156 OPEN Monday to Saturday 9:30am - 5:30pm

On Saturday 5th July, Emmaus, Glasgow opened its new 10,000 square foot furniture store in the East End of the city, on Summer Street, Bridgeton, on the site of a former supermarket – making it the largest charity shop in Glasgow. ADDRESS 576 Dumbarton Road, Partick, Glasgow G12 6RH TELEPHONE 0141 342 4089 OPEN Monday to Friday 9am - 4:30pm, Saturday 10am - 4pm

Furniture staples at St. Leonard's Hospice, York. ADDRESS 12 York Road, Acomb, York YO24 4LU TELEPHONE 01904 781 576 OPEN Monday to Friday 10am - 4pm, Saturday 10am - 1pm

Table and chairs on the pavement outside The Action Group, Leith. ADDRESS 336 Leith Walk, Edinburgh EH6 5BR TELEPHONE 0131 555 1224 OPEN Monday to Friday 10am - 4pm, Saturday 11am - 5pm

Side table and dining set at the The Princess Alice Hospice, Kingston. ADDRESS 34-36 Old London Road, Kingston Surrey KT2 6QF TELEPHONE 020 8547 2710 OPEN Monday to Friday 9:30am - 4:30pm, Saturday 9:30am - 4pm

Goods on display at Wawrs Werdd Furniture Store ADDRESS Antur Waunfawr Cyf, Bryn Pistyll, Waunfawr Caernarfon Gwynedd LL55 4BJ TELEPHONE 01286 674 155 OPEN Monday to Friday 9am - 4pm, Thursday 9am - 6pm, Saturday 10am - 1pm (and all bank holidays).

Sofas on sale at St Catherine's furniture shop in Chorley. ADDRESS 61 Clifford Street, Chorley, Lancashire, PR7 1SE TELEPHONE 01257 241 800 OPEN Monday, Tuesday, Thursday, Friday and Saturday 10am - 4pm. Closed Wednesday.

Chairs on display to tempt passers-by outside West Kent YMCA, Tonbridge. ADDRESS 30 High Street, Tonbridge, Kent TN9 1EJ TELEPHONE 01732 367 764 OPEN Monday to Saturday 10am - 5pm.

United Kingdom
New Zealand $3.75
Canada $4.95
U.S.A. $4.95

VINTAGE & RETRO

Barnardo's Vintage
- Grassmarket, Edinburgh

Barnardo's provides direct support to children, young people
and their families through 394 projects at home, school and
in the local community.

Open since early 2007, Barnardo's Vintage, is located at the bottom of Victoria
Street in the historic Grassmarket area of Edinburgh. It is the city's first vintage
charity shop and the first specialist Barnardo's venture established nationwide.
One other stand-alone vintage shop temporarily existed in London's Carnaby
Street, when the charity took over a free shop unit for a short period leading
up to Christmas 2007 – a project for which Grassmarket's manager Marie
Wallis was invited to act as consultant. Following the success of Edinburgh's
Stockbridge 'Vintage' department, Barnardo's Vintage was pushed forward.
Marie Wallis now oversees both Edinburgh shops.

Open seven days a week, the shop stocks a wide range of period clothing for
men and women, accessories, jewellery and bric-a-brac to suit the discerning
tastes of the younger population of Edinburgh. Strands of recognisable
memorabilia from popular culture across the decades have been amassed to
form this vintage nest. An Americana theme is evoked by the Johnny Cash
album playing on the stereo and a dominating poster image of Elvis Presley
high up on the wall. The lack of natural light and the orange glow from several
free-standing lamps around the room in lieu, transports the daytime shopper
into a state of suspended animation, along with the merchandise. Everything
in the shop that is not pinned to the wall is for sale. 1950s suits, 1960s mini
dresses and 1970s T-shirts pack out the rails. All staff and volunteers have
a good knowledge of vintage clothing and styles. There is a 'wants' list in
the shop for customers looking for specific items. Bebo and MySpace profile
pages attract a younger clientele.

All the merchandise is sourced from the local area. Other Barnardo's
shops in the city routinely send their dated garments to Grassmarket and
in addition Marie and her staff actively trawl the fellow Barnardo's shops
for items that would suit and sell at the boutique. Aware that some of the
other shops were ragging their vintage donations, either because they were
not aware of the potential value or because they recognised that they did
not have the right clientele to whom to market these goods, Marie set about
educating staff on how to identify collectable garments and fashionable styles
and gaining their support for her venture. It soon became apparent that she
was able to select her entire stock just from the ragbags of the other shops.

There is no standard branding in any part of the shop, deliberately
obscuring its charity status. As a result the shop receives very little in the
way of doorstep donations. Intended to work in this way, it uses solely
the charity's surplus stock to reduce its waste, simplify administration and
minimise storage requirements and manpower to dispose of inadequate or
unsuitable garments. Barnardo's Vintage differs from a normal charity shop

in its turnover time, with merchandise lasting eight weeks as opposed to the usual two or three before it is reconsidered, put into storage, passed on to the Stockbridge or Nicholson Street shops with vintage sections or disposed of. If the clothes go into storage, usually upstairs in the larger Stockbridge shop, they are brought out again after some months and will eventually sell.

The shop has full autonomy on pricing and Marie defines her own pricing structure, with a much higher price point than other Barnardo's shops. During the seasonal festivals the Vintage shop takes a sharp rise in profits and can float on this for the rest of the year. The Grassmarket site was carefully chosen because of the area's long-established connection with antiques, in order to exploit its customer base. 'Our prices are higher because care has been taken over the sourcing and presentation. Pre-sorting goods, in theory, increases the odds of finding something you want to buy. It is a time consuming business and we have to charge the extra to cover that cost,' explains Marie. A keen charity shopper herself, she realises that as manager for Barnardo's she is, to an extent, at odds with her personal interests in charity shopping.

People are now more than ever aware of the common value of goods, which may change throughout their lifespans, and have become brokers of their own belongings through auction sites like eBay. The shops receive less genuine vintagewear than they once did, as a result. Around five per cent of the stock here is pre-1950s and the particularly desirable labels are rare. Over the last few months the items that have stood out include a vintage Missoni top, and a YSL and a Chanel bag. At the moment it has some particularly special linen, sent from the Gorgie shop. A pre-1940s tiered cotton underskirt and silk robes from around the same period are both priced at £35. Ongoing celebrity endorsement of vintage clothing, along with a genuine concern for the environment in the fashion industry, has contributed to a sustained demand for this type of venture and the fact that the profits go to charity further enhances its reputation.

ADDRESS 116 West Bow, Edinburgh EH1 2HH TELEPHONE 0131 225 4751 OPEN Monday to Wednesday 10:30am - 5pm, Thursday to Saturday 10:30am - 6pm, Sunday 12pm - 5pm

Traid - Westbourne Grove, London

TRAID (Textile Recycling for Aid and International Development) is a charity committed to protecting the environment and reducing world poverty through recycling, delivering educational programmes and campaigning within the UK.

TRAID is a pioneering social enterprise that brings together environmental action and sustainable development in an exemplary way. The charity aims to make each of its outlets a destination shop, by selling a specific product type appropriate to the location. Close to Portobello Market, the Westbourne Grove shop offers some sought-after vintage and specialist clothing as well as the charity's award-winning recycled fashion label, TRAIDremade.

Founded in 2000, under the authority of Paula Kirkwood, TRAIDremade designers follow the fashion trends available on the high street, although they are working exclusively with donated materials and each piece is an original. According to the charity, every year in the UK 900,000 million items of clothing, shoes and accessories, weighing in at 1.3 tonnes, are thrown away. TRAIDremade saves textile waste from landfill and aims to provide an alternative style to cheap, identikit fashion on the high street. The label gives torn and stained clothing a new lease of life by mixing, matching, ripping, cutting, sewing and printing to achieve a DIY look that has now been widely reproduced/replicated by young fashion concession stores such as Topshop as well as other charity trading company concessions. Old shorts and flock curtains become a pair of high-waisted trousers or a torn skirt is transformed by use of appliqué. Having successfully showcased its clothing line at the Alternative Fashion Week, the label is now available in TRAID's Brighton, Brixton, Shepherds Bush and Wood Green shops.

The majority of rail space in this Portobello shop is dedicated to retrowear and vintage examples of both designer and high street brand names, from Sonia Rykiel to Marks and Spencer. TRAID appears to have set its filter level higher than most charity shops and all the clothes are of a consistently superior quality. This is made possible by the fashion expertise of the sorting staff who hand pick the best clothing for sale as well as the team of designers who provide their skills at customizing garments to create exclusive pieces from the rag bags.

The front window is dressed with brightly-coloured, theatrical combinations of clothes and the costumes are accessorised with hats, scarves, bags and belts, which constitute contemporary high street reproductions of historical silhouettes. Nevertheless, the shop inside comprises a decent selection of 70s and 80s clothes, some of which have recognisable labels and others from obscure boutique brands, from the international fashion capitals. To the right side of the shop there are men's shoes, trousers and coats in front of the changing rooms. To the left, there are women's accessories and coats, before the till counter. At the back, there is a rail of coats, in preparation for the approaching winter season. Throughout the middle of the shop there are several low rails of jumpers, tops, T-shirts, shirts and jackets.

Around the walls, a series of posters present professionally-styled fashion imagery, familiar to readers of contemporary fashion magazines, which promote the TRAID brand. The young manager of the shop is impeccably and fashionably dressed and sorts and prices clothes in the back room of the shop, systematically hanging the garments on the rails as she goes. I enquire about the prices, asking whether they are reduced after a period of time. After two weeks, I am told, unsold items are moved on to another TRAID branch and perhaps re-valued according to the sales potential of that particular shop. I buy an eiderdown-filled Moncler jacket for its fixed price of £39.99.

ADDRESS 61 Westbourne Grove, London W2 4UA TELEPHONE 020 7221 2421 OPEN Monday to Saturday 10am - 6pm, Sunday 11am - 5pm

Cancer Research UK - Camden, London

Cancer Research UK is the world's leading independent organisation dedicated to cancer research, supporting research into all aspects of cancer through the work of more than 4,500 scientists, doctors and nurses.

Cancer Research UK is one of the largest charity retailers with over six hundred shops across the country. As well as bringing in a range of new goods to its programme, the trading company has introduced a nationwide directive for a cohesive vintage identity in many of its shops. This Camden branch is just one example and conveniently taps into the passing trade of visitors to Camden Market, one of London's largest and most established second-hand markets. On market days, Camden Town is an entry-only underground station and many people leave the area by Mornington Crescent station, passing a string of six charity shops en route, including Cancer Research.

The concentration of charity shops along Camden High Street makes this stretch a viable destination for second-hand shopping in itself. Competition amongst the shops clearly encourages creativity in their presentation. All of the shops have, to a greater or lesser degree, styled themselves on sub-culture themes, with 'punk' being the currently popular street-style to revisit.

To capture the attention of young shoppers with vintage tastes this shop has put together a quirky new window display every few weeks, hinting at its retro selection and vinyl record collection inside. It recently orchestrated a 'live model' window display for a day, with attractive young girls posing in fashionable outfits assembled by the shop's manager. Some of the clothes are new and today the window is unconventional, with a reflective silver sheet on the ground augmenting and dispersing the rainbow of colours and patterns of the garish 'retro' garments. The clothes are hung on hangers that have been covered in leopard print fabric The window is filled with customised detritus, including a cartoon-comic decoupage suitcase. Advertisements for various products in the shop are written in paint on vinyl records and down the legs of a pair of jeans, pinned to the wall. The shop makes no secret of the customers it aims to attract to bring in new income. Nor does it seem to worry about alienating particular divisions of its existing clientele. Prices appear to be comparable to those of the market stalls up the road and potentially lucrative to the charity shop.

The 'retro' area of the shop is distinguished by a highly patterned floral fabric backdrop. One long rail of garments is coordinated by colour, graduating from browns and oranges on to turquoise shades and unsettled with bursts of a gaudy pattern. Some of the clothes are new but contribute the appropriate atmosphere to the collection, with many designs reflecting an eastern influence, representing popular styles of the 1960s and 1970s. The fabrics are mostly synthetic but there are some garments made from quality textiles, which together command a similar price that is generally more expensive than the rest of the clothes in the shop. A polyester zipped robe is £7.50. I find an YSL skirt in a provincial French stripe, slubbed Thai silk for £24.99. Around the rest of the shop there are several carefully retro-styled mannequins adorned with fluorescent wigs. Collaged graphic 'Retroagogo' signs are placed amongst the collections for added promotion of this assumed identity.

To help source stock for the 'retro' department, the shop relies on the assistance of other Cancer Research UK shops in the area, which collect stock and then forward this onto the branch with the specialist collection. I offer the Camden shop an old but functioning film camera and despite not selling electrical goods it accepts the item to use as a prop, presenting it as a 'donation item', to sell 'as seen' for a reasonable offer.

Under the terms of the leases, Cancer Research UK is obliged to repair and redecorate most of its shops every five years, in accordance with other high street retailers. In cases where it is not a stipulation of the lease, the charity takes into consideration many factors, such as the performance of the shop, before it undertakes a refit. 'The refurbishment of a shop helps to improve our high street presence, dispel the myths that sometimes surround charity shops and attract more support within the local community by providing a more pleasant shopping experience,' says Karlene McFarlane, Trading Communication and PR Executive for Cancer Research.

ADDRESS 81 Camden High Street, London NW1 7JL TELEPHONE 020 7383 5910 OPEN Monday to Saturday 9:30am - 5:30pm, Sunday 11am - 5pm

Salvation Army - Princes Street, Central London

The Salvation Army is a church charity and one of the largest, most diverse providers of social services in the UK after the government, demonstrating its Christian principles through social welfare provision.

The Salvation Army Trading Company Limited (SATCoL) operates a number of charity shops across the country, managed centrally from its Wellingborough headquarters. A further group of shops are run by divisional headquarters or local centres, but this particular branch next to Regent Hall, the Salvation Army Church, is one of the Trading Company's most successful outlets. This used to be a bargain price charity shop spread over two floors of a tall, terraced townhouse building behind Oxford Circus. It is London's most central charity shop and one of only a handful around the city's main shopping high street, Oxford Street, with the others gathered together on Goodge Street.

Despite its proximity to the main retail hub, the charity shop's immediate setting is a quiet side street with significantly less passing traffic. It is continuously mentioned in guides, however, and has established a regular customer base. Its identity has changed tack over the years, for a long time withstanding change and retaining the idiosyncrasies of an old-world charity shop. Some years ago it received a refit as part of SATCoL's overall move to upgrade their outlets and try out new marketing ideas. The stock has been revised and restyled and the interior has expanded with simple functional fittings, although the prices of the goods remain relatively modest.

The ground floor shop has been extended back into its depths and takes on a distinctly 'retro' thrust, encouraged by past publicity advertising its theatrical and occasional vintage finds, especially in the desirable new arena of 80s vintage. The overall visual impression gives it away as such, with bright colours and gaudy patterns coordinated together across the rails. Individual pieces have been extracted to hang around the top of the walls, emphasising style references of the past. The familiar Marks and Spencer 'gold standard' has been upgraded to the M&S Autograph range. There are some designer labels scattered amidst the rails, including Maxmara, Ralph Lauren and Nicole Farhi, as well as a few vintage examples. A large jewellery cabinet, brimming with modern costume pieces, doubles up as the till counter opposite the entrance door.

A few years ago the Salvation Army trialed a shop format called Again, which rebranded a handful of strategically chosen shops across the country with branded carrier bags and fascia. After reviewing the concept, the charity decided not to continue with Again as standalone shops and to convert them back to the core chain. This shop escaped the experiment but for some time the charity has run various speciality enterprises from its first floor room, including a bookshop that was closed for long periods of time due to a shortage of volunteers. Now a new fashion label called Emmeline 4 Re has taken over the space. After graduating in fashion from the University of Northampton, Emmeline Child was offered a two-year salaried position linked to University College Northampton as part of a Knowledge Transfer Partnership – a Department of Trade and Industry sponsored initiative to promote recycling. Based at the large Salvation Army recyclers, Kettering Textiles in Wellingborough, Emmeline was asked to develop a recycling scheme called The Waste Textile to remodel and remake clothes from waste textiles and to create a range of marketable clothing. Increasingly these recycling points are being moved to places in the world where rates of pay are lower, absorbing the added transport costs.

Emmeline has been working with the trading and textiles groups since 2004 and, now based in the Portfolio Innovations Centre at University College of Northampton, she has launched her own brand. A new range of signature clothes has been showcased at Topshop's flagship Oxford Street store, one of a select group of young designers to have a concession. All profits from sales go to The Salvation Army.

Last year Emmeline 4 Re became an independent label and the concept of an 'ethical fashion boutique' was presented to The Salvation Army, Princes Street, to develop a selection of labels concerned with recycling and challenging the pervasive stereotype of ethical fashion design as unattractive or lacking in style. The collections were launched in Hanover Square in October, promoting the idea of 'responsible luxury'. The boutique, now open, is sparsely arranged with decorative artwork and styled objects, augmented with buttons and scraps of cloth and made exclusively for the shop. Also on offer are innovative and sustainable product design ideas such as a Trevor Baylis wind-up light and an upholstered chair made out of a shopping trolley.

Emmeline's collection is one hundred per cent recycled, including the trimmings and buttons. Wool is cut into panels and not re-spun. The recycled 'look' focuses on pattern and prints and utilises the exuberant qualities of retro garments. A challenge is presented to the designers who are only able to make a couple of items at a time from scrap material. This restricts the label from going nationwide because it would not be able to fulfill demand. Supplementing the signature collection is Feng Ho's eveningwear that uses textiles such as bamboo, soy and organic silk as well as surplus rolls of fabric from British textile warehouses. Fabrics are hand printed and dyed using plant extracts to ensure that each garment is one of a kind, in subtle variation. Skirts and dresses are panelled and folded to give classic shapes a quirky twist. The labels qualify their claims of sustainability and 'environmental studio practice' by citing approval from London Remade and the Eco Design Project.

ADDRESS 9 Princes Street, London W1B 2LQ TELEPHONE 020 7495 3958
OPEN Monday to Saturday 10am - 6pm

Retromania, FARA - Pimlico, London

FARA charity shops generate income that is vital to the charity's work in Romania.

Retromania specialises in retro avant-garde and designer clothing as well as vintage pieces and memorabilia. Situated in the heart of London's Victoria it provides accessible stock for the city's television, film and theatre industries. Named in 2006 in the *Evening Standard* newspaper as one of the top five second-hand shops in London and by *Time Out* magazine as a 'creative hotspot' for art students, it has gone on to establish itself as a destination shop for the fashion press and the avid collector of retro clothing. Of course this is not a new role for the charity shop, which has, as a creative outlet, historically provided a unique resource for out-of-sync style and music. Together with the subsequent boom in the mainstream popularity of vintage clothing, this shop has recognised an opportunity to adapt itself to the niche market.

Its neighbour, Cornucopia, a few doors down on Upper Tachbrook Street, is an institution for second-hand and vintage clothing and costume but it is currently in the 'final reductions' stage of a closing down sale. Also in the business of recycling, Retromania has the added advantage of charitable status that it hopes will help it to survive the foreboding economic slump.

Co-manager Judy Gard is passionate about the clothes that she sells in the shop and the importance of salvaging them from the likelihood of ragging. She believes that much of our precious cultural heritage continues to be lost to the ubiquitous charity shop culture that readily rags any garment in need of repair or showing signs of wear. Although rags can often be recycled she is critical of the waste, particularly of natural fibres, when reuse represents a far more ecological proposition. She shows me an example of a severely pilled Biba sweater, priced at £25 for its historical value. She points out that in another charity shop it would more than likely have been ragged but here it is respected as an cultural artefact with potential for study in its construction, pattern or for repair.

Judy began to build a collection of vintage and contemporary designer clothing in 1995, when she ran a regular FARA charity shop that is now a speciality FARA Kids shop on nearby Tachbrook Street. She describes being attracted instinctively to the fabrics and shapes of the more unique items that came in to the shop and she had an idea that they might be more valuable to the charity than the average donation. A volunteer assistant with an intimate knowledge of fashion confirmed her collection as both historically important and highly valuable. The shop realised its potential to incorporate a 'vintage' room and FARA's first specialist shop, Retrospective, was launched, dedicated exclusively to selling the clothes in a showcase context. In 2003, the shop moved to its current address, and was renamed 'Retromania' in reference to its fundraising cause, for Romanian orphans.

At Retromania, 'vintage' constitutes anything from the 60s and earlier and finishes in the early 70s. The 'new vintage' is from the 80s and accounts for most of the stock available. There are more modern pieces too, some contemporary silhouettes and several period pieces made specifically for the theatre, as well as ethnic and traditional costume. Selected items can be hired at the manager's discretion. Pricing is governed by how hard it is to acquire the pieces and a premium is naturally attached to garments from periods with slim pickings. Vintage pieces have found their way less frequently to the shop. 'People don't give away vintage any more. It's become so popular now and, with the exposure, people know the value and hold on to it or sell it on eBay,' Judy comments. The shop receives little in the way of doorstep donations because it is not obviously a charity shop. It depends instead on its FARA partners to extract their most valuable stock for the specialist shop, where it can achieve a higher sale price.

Retromania holds seminars for the other shops, to educate staff on what not to rag. Judy points out that the minimum wage is not likely to attract individuals with specialist knowledge to the business unless employees have what she empathetically describes as 'an interest in paraphernalia'. It is hard to acquire staff at any level because the shop cannot offer well-paid positions. There is, however, the incentive of training and many volunteers who have used their time at the shop to acquaint themselves with the fashions and draw on Julie's expertise have gone on to get good jobs.

On the rails opposite the till counter there are undoubtedly some fine examples of designer goods throughout the decades; an immaculate Courreges wool suit from the 60s, a YSL skirt and jacket from the 70s and Ungaro and Chanel coats from the 80s. There is an extensive collection of accessories to match from both prominent and obscure vintage boutique labels, which are displayed in numerous tall glass cabinets around the shop. First edition books and period props, such as 78rpm records and record players, along with other mechanical equipment, such as projectors, telephones and cameras, help to place the attire within its historical context. The shop faces a dilemma over society's rapidly changing attitude to fur and against the need to make money for the charity. Judy recognises that selling any kind of fur gives it currency and perpetuates its fashion status. By displaying fur donations the shop opens itself up to attacks from animal rights groups but pieces that are over a certain age are nonetheless tentatively put out on sale.

Judy hopes that she has managed to maintain her own principles in the running of the shop. In return for working on behalf of the charity for so many years and contributing to the success of the venture she is able to use her discretion in pricing and in the way that the shop is presented. 'The manager has to be able to give their personality to the shop,' she says. She feels strongly that there must be a middle line on pricing, on the basis that a generous attitude should be encouraged in the shop. It is important to her and other staff that they maintain a reputation for being a reasonably priced shop. Judy just chose to sell three Chanel handbags for significantly less than the amount she had been advised upon. Nonetheless, she points out, they made over £400 for the charity and increased the shop's turnover rate.

Providing another example of this willingness to maintain affordable prices, a customer comes in to the shop and tries on a lavish showpiece silk kimono, priced at £200. Judy asks the woman what she feels she can afford and offers to take her telephone number and give her first refusal on the purchase for one week. Judy is very clear that she does not accept customers pushing for a discount but appears to practice a means-tested policy, filtered through her experience and intuition. She prefers to keep the valuable pieces on the shop floor than to sell them through the auction houses.

The sale rail outside is designed to attract passing interest. A set of traffic lights illuminate the words 'Stop, look, shop' and a giant pair of 50s spectacles have been cut out of MDF wood, sprayed gold and suspended from the draped open curtain doorway to the back of the shop. There is a box full of wigs for £5 each. Vintage tights and stockings in a seemingly modern colour palette together with a series of vintage *Vogue* dress patterns represent the full circle of fashion since the 1960s. Seminal counter-culture fiction titles like Douglas Coupland's *Generation X* cost £1, chosen to suit the mood and brandished for sale on a melamine-top table outside. The shop holds promotional evenings for the public at least three times a year and it has recently launched its own website on which Internet users can browse an ever-increasing wardrobe of retro designer and classic pieces, vintage collectables and chic avant-garde creations. Items can be purchased by telephone or by visiting the Pimlico shop itself.

ADDRESS 6 Upper Tachbrook Street, Pimlico, London SW1V 1SH TELEPHONE 020 7630 7406 OPEN Monday to Saturday 10:30am - 6pm, Sunday 11am - 5pm

Oxfam Vintage - Preston, Lancashire

Oxfam is a development, advocacy and relief agency working to put an end to poverty worldwide.

Oxfam Vintage is located on Friargate in Preston and it is one of a series of branches that the charity identifies as part of its 'Originals' scheme of shops around the UK, in nearby Manchester and Liverpool and just further afield in Leeds, York, Rochester and Nottingham.

As I enter the shop The Prodigy's *Music For The Jilted Generation* is playing, which coincidentally is the album I have just bought on cassette tape from Age Concern, to play on my car stereo. The music lends a lively and rebellious atmosphere to the shop and two members of staff who I perceive to be a fashionable young manager and her assistant are sorting through garments at the till and systematically hanging them on the appropriate rails whilst they discuss the recent gigs that they have attended.

The Vintage shop is clearly geared towards to the city's student population and seems to be the only outlet in the town for 'alternative' fashions, selling a comprehensive collection of clothes that represent every identifiable subculture that has been commercially exploited over the last sixty years. 'Punk' is sold back to the youth in the form of leather biker jackets, Breton striped T-shirts, narrow-cut suits and skinny ties for men, together with synthetic neon knitwear, trashy animal prints and mix-and-match styling for women.

There is also a large 'goth' section at the back of the shop selling the fetishised garments that were historically sourced from the legendary youth-style boutiques, such as Hyper Hyper in London. Black leather and white gauze, crushed velvet in scarlet and purple, red lace and black fishnet, PVC and patent all constitute a somewhat stereotypical jumble of items available to this group.

Classic designs are offered in abundance. A substantial amount of Levi jeans dating from the 1940s fills a circular rail – a staple of any large urban market stall. Prices range from £10 to £65. Immaculate Windesmere wool cardigans are £25. Vintage 80s high street brand shoes are consistently priced £12 a pair. There are plenty of accessories for dressing up in the way of bags, shoes, ties, cravats, hats, scarves and gloves, all at disposable fashion prices. The individual areas of clothing, tailored to specific themes, are treated to a styled contextual backdrop of props and displays that showcase the pre-sorted clothing as an example of the best vintages of the decades.

I look out for the genuine vintage labels that the shop's name suggests I might find here. When I ask the manager what she believes to define an authentic vintage piece, she corrects me, saying in an ironic tone, 'It's not "vintage" any more, it's "archive"' – a term that has either been adopted by the charity's marketing team or quoted from current popular journalism on the subject. She goes on to clarify the differentiation between 'vintage and 'retro': 'It's very hard to get 50s things now. Anything from the 60s onwards is easy to get hold of. "Vintage" roughly constitutes anything pre-1960s. The rest is retro fashion – inherently less rare and therefore less valuable.'

Applying this definition, I continue to look around the shop for genuine vintage labels, and find that there are a few, although not many. The manager explains that she prefers not to have too many vintage items on the shelves because they do not achieve anywhere near their potential value and she prefers to let Oxfam sell them online, through its auction sites. 'Some people think it should be cheaper because it's Oxfam, so I can't sell "vintage" for anything like the price it is worth,' she explains.

The shop gets a delivery once a week from the Oxfam depot in Huddersfield, of clothes picked especially to sell in this shop. Local donations are frequent too but the public brings everything and anything to the shop, rather than recognising it as a specialist shop. 'I just had a donation of five bin-bags of teddies and my tiny back room is over-spilling,' the manager exclaims, 'but I don't like to turn anything down for Oxfam, so I take it.' Excess or unsuitable merchandise is sent back to Huddersfield on the delivery van.

The charity shop has also recently started a new initiative, inviting Year Two Fashion Promotion students to work with Oxfam Vintage to promote its special fashion collection. Helen Warner once worked in Preston's Vintage shop and developed an expertise in fashion's historical key pieces dating back as far as the 1920s. She has now set up her own business, Defraye, designing and selling 'cool but ethical designer wear'.

ADDRESS 127 Friargate, Preston PR1 2EE TELEPHONE 01772 254 870
OPEN Monday to Saturday 10am - 5pm, Sunday 12pm - 4pm

The vintage rail at the Home Farm Trust (HFT) shop, Buxton. ADDRESS 61 Spring Gardens, Buxton Derbyshire SK17 6BJ TELEPHONE 01298 2334 OPEN Monday to Saturday 9am - 5pm

The only charity shop in this area, Mind, Stoke Newington builds up a collection of 'vintage' and 'retro' items to put out all together for sale, constituting a vintage section that features whenever stock permits. ADDRESS 11 Stoke Newington Church Street, London N16 0NX TELEPHONE 020 7812 9210 OPEN Monday to Saturday 9am - 5pm, Sunday 11am - 4pm

Many of the Helen & Douglas House shops have 'browse and coffee' book sections. Helen & Douglas House, Oxford also has a notable vintage area that constitutes a pair of rails of 80s vintage examples of well-known designer brands and eveningwear as well as a few older pieces. ADDRESS 158 Cowley Road, Oxford OX4 1RW TELEPHONE 01865 249 988 OPEN Monday to Saturday 10am - 5.30pm

The 'Retro & Interesting' rail at Bagpuss Children's Hospice, Edinburgh. Much of the interesting bric-a-brac and retro label clothing is channelled into the Tollcross branch of the Hospice of Hope charity. ADDRESS 62 Home Street, Tollcross, Edinburgh, Midlothian EH3 9NA TELEPHONE 0131 229 9696 OPEN Monday to Saturday 10am - 5pm

Worthing and District Cat's Protection, Worthing sells its own cat-themed products, such as tote bags, made of strong PVC-coated cotton and in colourful designs, tea-towels made from Irish linen and practical pet care items as well as the usual donated bric-a-brac. The shop also maintains a vintage rail as long as stocks allow this ADDRESS 35, Rowlands Road, Worthing West Sussex BN11 3JJ TELEPHONE 01903 200 332 OPEN Monday to Saturday 10am - 4pm

Barnardo's Vintage, Edinburgh (see page 210).

Accessories
Gift
Electrical
& White Goods
Childrenswear
Art & Craft

The Thrift Shop, Birthlink - Bruntsfield, Edinburgh

The Birthlink's service users are adopted adults, birth parents of people adopted as children and their families, adoptive families, local authorities and voluntary adoption agencies. Other social care and health professionals may contact the service for advice.

One of two Birthlink charity shops, The Thrift Shop on Bruntsfield Links proudly presents itself as 'Scotland's oldest charity shop'. Everything in the shop is reused, admirably including the shop's carrier bags, hangers, shelving units and rails. Where there is a shortage of donated storage boxes, the shop makes do with cardboard boxes. Cleaning materials, paper and pens are also donated. The shop units themselves were acquired some years ago and so there are no rent costs. Price tags are one of the few things on which the shop has outlaid any of its profits.

The day-to-day running of the shops is taken care of by head office and, where it can, the charity relies on donated time and materials to maintain its retail activities. Any upgrade to the décor requires money that the charity simply does not have. There is no underlying psychology to this lack of change, but the public is perhaps more inclined to be generous if it believes that the maximum amount of proceeds from its donations is going to the charity, and such an outward sign of frugality may help the cause. This outward sign of prudence also indicates a tradition in a religious ethic, convincing visitors of a trustworthy operation. Shop manager Dorothy MacAlister appreciates the policy of resourcefulness. She believes the charity shop provides an excellent means of recycling, growing rapidly in its importance to society and gaining exposure for itself as a mediator of this vital process, as it continues to raise money for its chosen cause. This shop does not refuse any type of castoff, even taking in rags for their shredding value.

As well as being the oldest charity shop in Scotland, Dorothy believes that The Thrift Shop is also the cheapest. There is always a '10p' box of goods outside the door, as an irresistibly priced curiosity, as well as cheap paperback novels, to lure in the passer-by. Such negligible prices tokenise a monetary transaction, as not only can 'freebies' evoke suspicion but also the rule of shop breaks down entirely without some sort of financial exchange. Dorothy tends to give away any of these items for free, however, to those who look like they might be in need. When the weather turns cold she will often tuck a pair of socks in to a pair of shoes being purchased. Winter hats and scarves are £1. Coats are priced at between £5 and £10. With the more frivolous items, a little more might be added to the value but if the item has a practical use then the cost is kept low, giving everyone an unofficially means-tested share in the spoils of donations.

Some may not find beauty in the purely functional, and compared to the pervasive national brand of charity shop, the shop is scruffy, but it serves its purpose very well. It is traditional in its content of clothes and bric-a-brac. One particularly attractive feature is a large antique retail cabinet of hosiery drawers, behind the counter, which stocks women's hosiery, men's socks and an array of accessories, such as belts, ties, hats and scarves. The front window, partitioned with a lace curtain, is always presented neatly.

The shop fulfills a niche role in the local community. The staff takes extreme care in handling donations to respect peoples' belongings and their emotional content. 'If you take time to consider the value of an item then the benefactor will be happy to give away more of their possessions in the future,' Dorothy explains. She often asks the customer what *they* think their donation is worth and what the shop should charge for it. For the more unusual items this is an efficient way of pricing. It also ensures that the customer feels valued. 'You don't want to give a cashmere jumper to a charity shop to find they've slapped a £3 tag on it if it's worth £20. If someone has gone to the bother of lugging a set of golf clubs to the shop they want to see their full worth realised, for the charity and for the sake of the items themselves,' she continues. The charity is grateful to its local patrons, without whom it could not function, and endeavours to reward them by keeping prices down and being open to negotiation on value.

Birthlink has a strict policy on new goods. It does not buy in new items to sell through the shops on principle, and a local company in the way of end-of-line products will have donated anything new that might appear on the shelves. Dorothy feels that charities which do so fail to acknowledge the potential for peripheral damage to small businesses in local communities. She cites the Northumberland village of Casterton where small businesses have struggled to compete with the charity shops selling new goods at knockdown prices. Some charity shops are beginning to take full advantage of their purchasing power as conglomerates. Dorothy regards this as mercenary because the shops already have the advantage of reduced rates.

Birthlink's second shop is situated on Gilmore Place nearby, across the road from the King's Theatre.

ADDRESS Birthlink, 6 Bruntsfield Place, Edinburgh EH10 4HN TELEPHONE 0131 229 4646 OPEN Monday to Saturday 9:30am - 5:30pm

Liphook Care Shop, The Bordon And Liphook Charity - Liphook, Hampshire

The Bordon and Liphook Charity distributes the profits from its two charity shops to those in need living in Bordon, Liphook and the surrounding areas.

Even though there are now one or more charity shops in every town and village in the country, the Liphook Care Shops are unusual in that they exist solely to raise funds, through donation of goods, to feed back into the local community. Funds are distributed by way of grants given to individuals who have been referred to the charity by professionals, as well as to local organisations and charities. The trustees are prepared to respond immediately to emergency cases and the cases they work on are numbered rather than named to avoid exposing the identity or address of applicants, which is important in maintaining an unbiased service within such an intimate framework.

As well as making their profits available for the local community the two shops also provide affordable clothes and household items to local residents. As a 'Community in Action' charity, the Care Shops fulfill two essential roles for the people of their respective Hampshire villages. The Liphook shop shares an optimal trading position, on Station Road, with a Cancer Research shop opposite. The local supermarket closed last year, which has dramatically reduced foot-flow past the shops, but the loyalty of its customers as well as the continuous generosity of its donors has meant that Liphook Care has managed to maintain its objectives in providing reasonably priced goods to the public and returning all the proceeds to the locality.

I ask the two volunteers in the shop if there is any competition between the charity shops, which appear to confront each other awkwardly on this barren limb of the village. 'People think Cancer Research is more up-market and sometimes prefer to give their stuff there. A person might also have had experience of cancer and choose to give to a cancer charity,' says one of the ladies. The two outlets are very different. Cancer Research is a small generic scion of its re-branded flagship stores whereas the Liphook Care shop remains a quaint stronghold in the ragtag style of charity shop. It is inevitable that Liphook Care finds it difficult to compete for visibility against such a high profile charity and it is interesting to hear that its interests and those of its immediate locale are not outweighed by the advantage of stature within the industry.

I watch three people pull up in cars outside and take large bin bags in to Cancer Research. I ask one donor why she has in this instance favoured one shop over the other and she tells me that the bags she is donating are full of left-over goods from a recent Cancer fundraising fete and so she felt this shop to be the appropriate recipient. She says she gives to both shops, usually without prejudice, although sometimes she finds one has too many items and takes her donation to the other. I ask her if she is familiar with the Liphook Care cause and although she is aware it is a charity shop she is not sure as to the cause of its fundraising. Perhaps customers are more willing to patronise a charity shop when they are familiar with its charitable aims than is generally assumed.

An article from the local *Herald* newspaper, named 'Charity Starts with a Bargain,' is pinned up by the counter at the Liphook Care Shop. It acknowledges the incentive required for charitable giving. 'Charity begins at home,' it reads. Those who know about the Liphook and Bordon Charity's mission continue to travel from within a wide radius to support the shop, which manages to achieve its fundraising targets. There is clearly a big effort made to keep the shop looking tidy and attractive. The volunteers are currently preparing for the 'Liphook in Bloom' competition. I see the shop is a winner of the 2006 award, marked by a presentation plate hanging on the wall by the counter.

All types of goods are stocked here, from the practical through to ornamental merchandise. There are bunches of knitting needles in the haberdashery section. Board games and toys, clothing, accessories, books, homeware and kitchen utensils share makeshift floor space with shelves of polished souvenir and occasion glassware. Another set of shelves is filled from floor to ceiling with VHS video tapes. A volunteer tells me a story about the promotional mascot, Dusty Bin, from the 1980s Saturday night television show *3-2-1* that was given to the shop to keep as a feature by presenter Ted Rogers (once a Liphook resident), but was sold on accidentally by an unwitting member of staff. The jewellery case in the counter top catches my eye. There is a lot of attractive costume jewellery, peppered with a few unique and vintage pieces. I buy a simple Victorian coral-bead necklace with hallmarked red-gold clasp for £3. A more ubiquitous gold cross and chain is marked at a premium £10.

ADDRESS 23 Station Road, Liphook, Hampshire GU30 7DW TELEPHONE 01428 727 211 OPEN Monday to Friday 9:30am - 4:30pm, Saturday 9:30am - 1pm

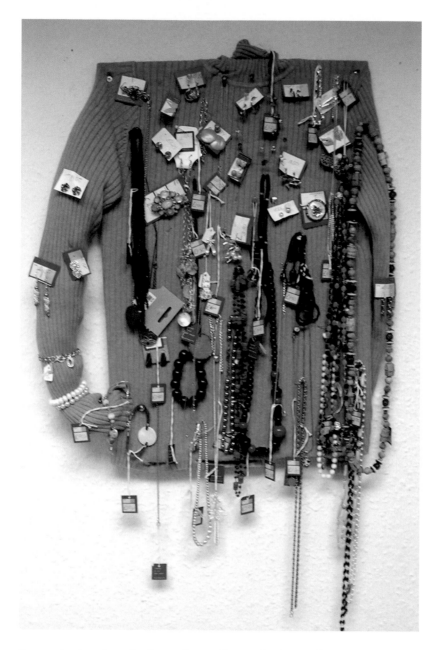

Innovative jewellery display at Cancer Research, Newcastle. Another Cancer Research in the city can be found at Saville Row, but this branch accepts furniture and maintains a retro section, currently reconstituting itself after a sell-out of stock. ADDRESS 61, Grainger St, Newcastle Upon Tyne, Tyne and Wear NE1 5JE TELEPHONE 0191 2305419 OPEN Monday to Saturday 9am - 5pm, Sunday 11am - 4pm

Books and clothes at Hospice of St Francis, Berkhamsted. (There is another St. Francis shop in Berkhamsted called Number Twenty at 20 Lower Kings Road, offering a selection of seasonal gift ideas and decoration for the home.) ADDRESS 274 - 276 High Street, Berkhamsted, Herts, HP4 1AQ TELEPHONE 01442 863 863 OPEN Monday to Saturday 9am - 5pm

Helen and Douglas House - The Covered Market, Oxford

The Hospice provides respite and end of life care for children and young adults with life-shortening conditions, as well as support and friendship for the whole family.

Oxford's Covered Market is discretely positioned behind the main pedestrian Market Street, attached to The Golden Cross shopping centre by a short walkway. These are two shopping experiences in sharp contrast to one another. The first is on the tourist map, although, when I ask for directions, both locals and tourists alike are unsure as to exactly where the Covered Market Halls are located. Once I find the site, I discover a satisfyingly eerie combination of genuinely old and 'old-fashioned' businesses that appear to capitalise on the quaint location. The market is housed in an impressively proportioned Georgian building, designed by John Gwynn, and despite the faded grandeur there is a vibrant atmosphere. Originally, the shops in this complex sold meat exclusively, but there is now on offer a diverse mix of 'stall' goods and services.

The Helen and Douglas House shop sits comfortably within this context. It is a dedicated gift shop, twinkling with fairy lights that are strung up around the windows, in the perpetual gloom of the covered walkways. The stock looks fresh and modern and is a mix of new, bought-in, donated and, most appealingly, hand-made goods. These include quilts (single £85, double £125), crocheted blankets, tea-cosies and a large amount of hand-knitted baby clothes that are made from the brightly coloured acrylic wool sold in the shop. The charity shop is unable to sell sheep's wool products because it would not be able to price them high enough to cover the cost of production. The same fact applies to the bedspreads and household textiles – natural yarns are more desirable and therefore demand a premium that the majority of customers are not prepared to pay. This anomaly between the unique, homemade product and economy on materials draws the products back from the luxury market and keeps them within the realm of gift goods.

Most of the greeting cards are also hand-made, donated to the shop or sold for cost price. There is plenty of 'Oxford' souvenir merchandise. In an age where home technology enables DIY production to a high standard the 'home-made' products here blend seamlessly with the bought-in, mass-manufactured ones. Printed T-shirts, mouse-mats, mugs and stationary are sold alongside more practical tools such as maps, guides and literature for the tourists. Old-fashioned floral prints make up aprons, peg-bags, placemats and pencil cases.

There is a small selection of second-hand bric-a-brac, arranged neatly over chrome-plated shelving units. The baby knitwear section is filled out with

donated baby clothes and children's wear. Facing this window selection is a portion of wall space displaying a large selection of second-hand costume jewellery that seems to be the main focus of customers' interest.

As well as providing a home collection service for larger items, the charity actively markets its shops as recycling hubs. Once donated stock has been pre-sorted, unsuitable items such as worn out clothing are sold on to other companies for reprocessing, which aim to provide good quality garments at a fraction of European prices for people in developing countries who would otherwise be unable to afford new clothes of this kind. Textiles are also recycled at a local level. The quilts, for example, are traditionally a product born of hardship and resourcefulness and are made here by reusing fabrics that have been donated to the shop. This demonstrates forward-thinking entrepreneurship on the part of the charity shop, in its attempt to adapt to its context and tap into the potential market for high quality gift items that preserve ethical values in a traditionalist context.

Helen and Douglas House also operates a dedicated furniture shop in Didcot and offers for sale a large selection of donated goods from its warehouse site shop in Grove. Its Cowley Road branch in East Oxford hosts a collection of vintage clothing and a dedicated book department (see 'Vintage & Retro').

ADDRESS 69-73 The Covered Market, Oxford, OX1 3DX TELEPHONE 01865 243 291 OPEN Monday to Saturday 8:30am - 5:30pm, Sunday 10am - 4pm

Fair Share, Immanuel Community Church – Soho, London

The Fair Share shop is a temporary retail business set up by the ICC 'for the sale of fair trade goods and other associated activities of the church.'

Fair Share opened its doors in 2005, transformed from an empty butcher's shop. The ceramic tiles have been spray-painted, new doors and a carpet have been fitted along with various shop fittings and display units.

Rents in the area are generally high and this is a prime shopping street in the centre of town. Westminster Council still owns this side of Berwick Street and as part of a major redevelopment plan of the area, the block was due to be demolished the following year. The local council offered the retail unit rent-free to the Immanuel Community Church so that it would be actively occupied rather than vacant, as it had been for several months. Local people and regular Berwick Street shoppers, as well as the market traders, have all showed their support and, three years on, a hold on redevelopment plans has kept Fair Share in business.

Fair Share is run by the ICC church, which has been in existence in Soho since 1987 and had a steady growth for a number of years, although since 1997 the numbers have dwindled and the small congregation now meets at its sister church in Covent Garden. Despite this, the church still has a strong reputation in Soho, established through many years of service in the local community, and now aided by these premises it maintains its profile with a sustained presence at street level.

Every church is a registered charity but this is not a conventional charity shop in that all its merchandise is new, bought in through Fair Trade suppliers to support and serve the purpose of fair trade. The only obvious charitable contribution is through its volunteer workforce, made up of ICC parishioners. One volunteer lives particularly close by and can therefore commit more time than most to the running of the shop, The manager, on several local committees, is also the church pastor.

The shop has enjoyed a favourable few years and has slowly built up the business, developing a strong relationship with its customers. Fair Share sells a range of handmade gifts and cards, as well as a selection of foodstuffs, including coffee and tea, made available by its main distributors, TraidCraft and Tearcraft. It continues to expand its range of suppliers to invite some smaller organisations to gain exposure for their products and new items are always being trialled. There are limits on how much Traidcraft or Tearcraft can sell and one way to help producers is to introduce them to other suitable buyers, in the fair trade movement or mainstream.

For Fair Share, the necessary experimentation on its stock purchases can be costly. It recently marketed a collection of clothes, especially for children, but it did not sell well. The volunteer I speak to explains that attempts to reduce clothing stocks to half the price, selling garments for as little as £8, could still not compete with unassailable competition from budget retail chains, all operating flagship stores on nearby Oxford and Regent Streets.

By buying one batch at a time, to test its popularity, the shop has established a core range of goods. Products that have proved most successful are the ornamental and decorative crafts, homeware, gifts and stationary. The volunteer believes that the woodwork sells particularly well because, she says, 'The English have forgotten how to do craft, but we still appreciate it. It's in us.' A 'Trash Chic' collection of recycled products made in Thailand from rice sacks is also selling very well, for between £6 for a notebook and £23 for a bag. More colourful bags and baskets are made from recycled wrapping and packaging. There is an extensive jewellery collection that fills a glass-topped cabinet in the centre of the floor and textiles, made by a 'Third World Women's Organisation', are displayed in the window, along with handmade glassware. All are accompanied by brief information about the craft and the various companies' production standards.

As well as the luxury and gift products there is also a small range of basic household provisions on sale, such as recycled toilet paper and ecological cleaning fluid. Tea and tea caddies, coffee and cafetières, fruit juice, chocolate, biscuits and snacks all carry a fair trade mark. The shop also stocks a limited range of local hand-made goods, such as knitted toys, and includes itself in the Wedgecard scheme that encourages people to shop locally, with the slogan 'Think local, shop local.' This is joined on posters around the walls with the headline: 'Consuming with a conscience.' Such a choice inevitably comes at a cost to the consumer, which makes this 'charity shop' not the usual opportunity for thrift but rather a conscious expenditure in the interests of others.

At the beginning of 2006, Fair Share was granted membership to the British Association of Fair Trade Shops (BAFTS). Oxfam is one of the country's largest fair trade retailers and stocks certified products in the majority of its shops across the country. Fair trade supports ethical and sustainable business practices and traditional craftsmanship. It aims to offer 'a better deal for small-scale producers in poor countries,' by achieving a fair and stable price for their product, developing a stronger position in world markets and a closer link between consumers and producers. It also promotes a greater respect for the environment.

A 'fair price' for the producer means that it not only covers the cost of production but also makes a profit to sustain a reasonable quality of life. Sometimes it might simply be a better wage. Fair Share cites, for example, Sheraj Gagi, a weaver in Bangladesh, whose wages increased by over forty per cent when he moved from a purely commercial employer to Aarong, a Traidcraft supplier. In other situations, a fair trade premium may fund developments for the producers or their community. It is critical that Traidcraft and Tearcraft buy from organisations that ensure that the benefits reach the original producers. These can be co-operatives, women's organisations, development projects or simply standard businesses, of varying sizes, as long as there is a clear benefit to the producer.

Of course, a fair trade organisation can only operate within the constraints of trade and has to make a sustainable profit for itself. International trade involves many processes, all of which have to be paid for in the final price (the cost of transport and marketing for a product, for example). It does not always have the benefit of the savings that can come when large volumes of a single product are involved. The advantages it creates are modest, yet significant, based on small percentage increases of the final price of a product or provision of wages and working conditions that are better than average in the locality. It also encourages workers' participation in ownership and decision-making and focuses on how a trade relationship is conducted. Other benefits include advance payments at low or no interest, design advice, market information, building the capacity of producers to understand the export market, a long-term commitment to a trading relationship and helping producers to increase their export markets. These differences may all, in the end, be more important to the producers than the price.

ADDRESS 102 Berwick Street, London W1F 0QP TELEPHONE 020 7287 8827
OPEN Monday to Saturday 12pm - 6pm

Hove YMCA - Hove, East Sussex

Support services for young people and families in the community, especially those isolated, homeless, excluded from school, experiencing family breakdown, poor mental health or drug and alcohol problems.

This YMCA shop, on one of the main roads linking Hove with Brighton, shares a commercial stretch with a few other local charity shops and has enough space to be able to specialise in electrical, electronic and white goods. It spans two large retail units, the second of which is shared between the white goods – ovens, fridges and freezers, for example – and a growing furniture collection. Clusters of lights hang from the ceiling. An array of table lamps perch along a deep shelf that runs high around the walls. The first half of the shop is stacked full of every kind of electrical household appliance, including compact music systems and separates, televisions, video and DVD players, portable amplifiers, musical instruments, microwaves, washing machines, vacuum cleaners, computers and kitchen and garden appliances.

Many of the items here might be considered retrograde. Widescreen and flat screen televisions, for example, are fast replacing the original square sets. However, the YMCA's stock reflects to some degree even the most advanced technology, as digital goods become more commonplace. The charity shop goods are suited to those people more interested in quality and proven longevity, as well as the principles of sustainability, than those who are simply concerned with keeping up with the current trends and owning the latest

products. Many of the older products on sale, the staff point out, are made with better quality components than their newer versions and it is only reasonable to expect that these goods might need some technical attention during their lifetime. Some customers also prefer the 'retro' designs of outdated products and an aesthetic or nostalgic motivation drives the purchase.

All appliances are PAT tested and fully functioning, repaired if necessary by a worthy team of technical experts to ensure that items not only meet regulations but will go on to last a second lifetime. Everything is certified to an industrial standard and comes with a thirty day guarantee. In many cases, the items have retained their original packaging and even their manuals. A lot of the appliances are displayed with the power switched 'on' in order to demonstrate the fact that they work – as well as particular qualities. This does not tally with the shop's environmentally-friendly identity but it is a policy, common to mainstream shops, that is considered necessary to attract buyers and secure the sale of such goods.

Due to the surge in affordable new technology over the last decade, enabling people to update and upgrade, household appliances are being replaced so rapidly that shops such as this have to work hard to keep up with donations. All the top brands are present on the floor. The staff can afford to be fastidious in the choice of items they consider to be fit for reuse, to sell on. Televisions are kept only if they have their remote controls. The shop also sells the cables, attachments and power supplies that are required to rig up the appliances at home, again mostly donated or stripped from other machines that were perhaps not suitable for reuse but are perfectly good for deconstruction and the recycling of parts.

The WEEE (Waste Electric and Electronic Equipment) Directive aims to address the issues brought about by the changing market and regulates businesses affiliated with waste disposal management. Since coming in to force in 2007, the YMCA must fulfill its obligations under this Environment Agency initiative. Through its recycling, reuse and treatment (de-pollution and preparation for disposal) programmes, the charity reports that it saves four hundred tonnes of landfill each year. Log sheets are approved by DEFRA (Department of Environment, Food and Rural Affairs) and other reuse networks.

The shop has now replaced its recycled white goods with newly manufactured appliances because, although the second-hand goods proved to be a huge success, the technicians could not fix them up quickly enough to keep them on the shop floor. The amount of work required to match them to regulations could not justify their low price, dictated by competition from large supermarket chains. Instead, the charity's trading company decided to buy in bulk brand new goods. The YMCA electrical shop is now selling these off at bargain prices so that the furniture section can grow and eventually dominate the business. Printed notices around the room assert that the products undercut the prices of companies such as Currys, Comet or Carter's by as much as twenty-five percent.

I decide to buy a kettle that is an exact replacement for an old one I once had that broke. It occurs to me that with electrical goods it is often cheaper to replace rather than repair them. I go on to calculate that if I had donated my broken kettle to the YMCA I could have then bought it back for around £5, fixed up, with a one month guarantee, essentially paying £5 for the electrical repair. In the past I have found it hard to find an electrician willing to fix such items because it has proved to be more economic to buy a very cheap replacement. Charity shops such as this one therefore represent a kind of long-term rental facility, which in turn maintains demand for and preserves professional roles in skilled labour.

The furniture sold here is provided by the charity's Amenity Site warehouse (see 'Emporium') and a team of van drivers collect from individual donors and house clearances in the local area to secure a high volume of stock. The advertisement on its postcards reads 'SAVE ME!...Save the environment. Recycle what you don't need.' Drivers distribute flyers on quiet afternoons and the charity also advertises online, through its website. The YMCA is a regionalised charity, allowing the individual branches to take on a local responsibility. Retail co-ordinator Mark Roberts ensures that the business has a direct relationship to the community in which it is operating, so that its interests are clearly the same as those of its local residents. The charity engages in volunteer programmes and training young people who have been ordered to undertake Community Service, as well as providing money for equipment and services for youth groups and projects.

ADDRESS 66 Blatchington Road, Hove BN3 3YN TELEPHONE 01273 776 868
OPEN Monday to Saturday 9am - 5pm

British Red Cross, Forfar, Angus. BRC sells second-hand furniture in a number of its shops across the UK, but this is one of three furniture and electrical charity shops. ADDRESS 128-130 East High Street, Forfar, Angus DD8 2ER TELEPHONE 01307 469 779 OPEN Monday to Saturday 9am - 5pm

In store display at St Francis Hospice Electrical Shop, Cranham. ADDRESS 125 Avon Road, Cranham, Upminster,Essex TELEPHONE 01708 222 777 OPEN Monday to Friday 9:30am - 4:30pm

Relate - Whitstable, Kent

Relate is the UK's largest provider of relationship counselling and sex therapy, also offering a range of other relationship support services.

Visitors have been coming to Whitstable in fluctuating numbers since the Canterbury and Whitstable railway first opened in 1830. The seaside town has earned a reputation for the influx of Londoners who have purchased second homes here, which has been blamed for pushing up the average house price. Boutique shops have emerged to service holiday residents and tourists and the independent traders have survived. Childrenswear is not a category of goods well catered for on the high street. However, clothing labels that are not associated with local retailers find their way to the town's charity shops and Relate makes a feature of its collection. This is not a speciality shop but it has a notable selection of toys and children's clothing that combined with a family-friendly atmosphere makes it a destination shop for parents. The charity overall is concerned with helping couples with difficulties in their relationships that more often than not involve children.

A large wicker basket on the shop floor contains garments for babies, from nought to eighteen months old. Clothing for a mix of ages is spread over two rails, with babies on one side and girls up to thirteen years on the other. The teenage collection is small and sells best during the summer months when it comprises beachwear and swimwear for girls who have reached an age that tends to be more particular in its tastes for regular daywear fashions. Yet another rail of children's clothes runs beneath a long upper stretch of both men and women's clothing. The idea is that 'mix and match' groupings generate customer interest in collections where there might not otherwise have been any. In the window, to the right side of the shop, cuddly toys cluster together, within reach of small children and the staff are relaxed about allowing playtime with the stock in the open space in the middle of the shop floor. There is also a modest choice of practical equipment, such as car seats, prams, pushchairs and highchairs.

Altogether this is a traditional charity shop that is designed to appeal to all ages and interests, stocking many different kinds of goods besides electricals. 'Out of ten people, I'm certain that eight could find something to buy in here,' says assistant manager Lorraine Pyle. The owner of a local fabric shop occasionally donates old stock and the outlet across the road frequently provides gift and souvenir items. A new charity shop is due to open in the town, bringing the total to eleven, and Relate is yet to find out whether the addition will affect its business.

The staff like to work with the other charities along the high street to send customers between their shops for specifically sought-after items. A cohesion of local business interests is enhanced by a sense of community spirit amongst retailers, symbolised by a mural on the wall directly outside the Relate shop that marks the occasion of the Royal Jubilee and depicts a piece of local history in its portrayal of the celebrations. A traditional red post box stands in front, where boxes of bric-a-brac and books are offered for browsing by the shop on trestle tables, and together with the painted imagery the whole scene invites a cosy nostalgia for the values of another era.

Whilst this is probably the biggest charity shop in Whitstable it has a 'tit and tat' content. Its appearance gives it several noteworthy advantages over its slicker competitors who have evidently invested more money in rebranding and redecoration. 'Locals feel comfortable knowing that we have our priorities in the right order. We direct as much money as possible to Relate and we make do and get by with what we've got to work with,' says Lorraine. Volunteers keep the shop clean and tidy and make a feature of its window displays. Customers testify to especially enjoying rummaging through the genuine mix of jumble at prices that seem to promise a bargain. Denise Johnstone has managed the shop for fifteen years and likes to be on familiar terms with her customers, ensuring that there is always something for the regulars, keeping stock moving and working hard to get new items out on to the floor each day.

Goods are priced for the locals. Due to the nature and profile of the charity, it is low on the donations list and this acts as a further invisible cap on pricing. A dress in the window is marked at a modest £4 and induces a passer-by to come in to the shop and tell the staff that it deserves a higher price. Encouraged by her comment, the staff add £20 to the value and the customer returns to buy it.

ADDRESS 44 Harbour Street, Whitstable, Kent CT5 1AH TELEPHONE 01227 266 175 OPEN Monday to Saturday 9:30am - 4pm

FARA Kids & Cafe - Earlsfield, London

'A family for those without' – FARA supports some of the most disadvantaged families in Eastern Europe.

Five minutes walk down Garrett Lane from Earlsfield overground train station, and passing en route a regular Fara charity shop selling the usual clothing and bric-a-brac range, is the Fara Kids and Café shop. One of four specialist Fara shops, this branch opened nearly two years ago to fill a well-identified gap in the market as the only childrenswear retailer in the area. Earlsfield is a residential suburb of London, growing rapidly in the demographic of young families in an upwardly mobile step towards wealthier neighbouring areas. The streets and cafés are busy with double-buggy traffic and the shop has been a success from the outset, with young parents, predominantly mothers, using it as a regular meeting place whilst their children play freely with the toys provided. Demand for good quality second-hand children's clothes remains high and the café, incorporated into the back of the shop, is popular, particularly in the afternoons.

Childrenswear is a booming sector of the clothing market, with cheaper clothes available and extended families and friends buying more clothes for new babies, far exceeding necessity. Children, especially young babies, grow out of their clothes so quickly that the garments on the rails here are, if not new, then in next-to-new condition. This makes the shop feel more like an upmarket children's boutique than a charity shop, which is likely to be a significant factor in the shop's success. Other charity shops that include a children's section have reported slow sales, commonly attributed to a persisting stigma: the belief that second-hand goods may be detrimental to a child's health and welfare. Budget retail shops, such as Primark, are also blamed, for their unbeatable prices. Repeated washing exposes the poor quality of cheap garments but the compromise is overridden by the lifespan requirements upon them. Their disposability becomes an acceptable feature because they are so quickly outgrown. For parents who look for better quality clothing and natural fibres, Fara *Kids* offers an extensive range at affordable prices. There are hand-knitted garments for sale, such as wool cardigans, hats and booties for as little as £3 and reductions are offered as an incentive to making multiple purchases.

Familiar and comforting icons of children's literature feature throughout the shop in the books and decor, conveying traditional values and conjuring fond childhood memories. Framed Winnie the Pooh prints hang in the window and the front room is minimal and styled to reflect current fashions in interior design, with cream-coloured walls and stripped wooden floorboards. Bedroom furniture supplements the standard shop rails. Two chests of drawers usefully compartmentalise a collection of baby garments,

such as babygrows, hats, mittens, booties, bibs, socks and tights. All ages are catered for, segregating gender, up to fifteen years, with the biggest selection of clothing consolidated for children ranging between eighteen months and four years old. A child safety gate bars the staircase down to a basement room that houses the shop's goods for babies and maternity wear. A range of pushchairs and buggies are available, costing from £20 to a maximum of £120 – all have been reduced to their present price. Highchairs, cots, slings and playmats are displayed around the floor. There is a small rail of maternity clothes along with a shelving unit stacked awkwardly with the remaining miscellany of blankets, baths and bottles for small babies.

The original back room of the building, extended by a further café room, is now the middle unit of the shop. There is a modern, spacious toilet and baby changing room. Toys are separated by type, which inevitably highlights the cultural conditioning of the sexes. Books are mixed in their topics and range from £1 to £3. Videos are 50p or three for £1. Costumes and masks have their own rail and there is a large shelf of board games and another presenting learning aid toys. Individual baskets of accumulated sets of toys, such as classic Lego pieces, are sold 'as seen'.

Dark wood vinyl flooring runs through this dark region of the shop to a bright extension room where the radio creates a lively atmosphere and seems to open up the shop to the outside world once again. A striking combination of red and white walls, five clean melamine tables and the café kitchen provide a fresh and inviting interior in which to take refreshment and pass the time. Natural light pours into a playroom annex, through a corrugated clear plastic roof, where toys, books and magazines for mothers are strewn around the floor. Leaflets on nutrition and activities for children are spread over the tables. Hot drinks are available and there is a coffee machine. The various toasted sandwiches and juices on offer are advertised on the menu board as well as healthy snacks, such as raisins, which are offered on the counter. A local cottage industry supplies homemade cakes. The café closes half an hour earlier than the shop, to make time for cleaning.

Other FARA Kids shops can be found in Pimlico, Clapham, Fulham and Teddington, although the Earlsfield branch is the only one to include a café.

ADDRESS 589 Garratt Lane, Earlsfield London SW18 4ST TELEPHONE 020 8879 7279 OPEN Monday to Saturday 9am - 5:30pm, Sunday 10am - 4pm

Toys, games and keyboards on display at the British Red Cross, Hedon
ADDRESS Watmoughs Arcade, Hedon, Hull, North Humberside, HU12 8EZ
TELEPHONE 01482 890 668 OPEN Monday to Saturday 9:30am - 5pm

Racks of children's clothing at the Salvation Army, Durham ADDRESS 58-62
North Road, Durham DH1 4SQ TELEPHONE 0191 383 1534 OPEN Monday
to Saturday 9:30am - 5pm

The Mill, Mind - Cowley Road, Oxford

The Mill is for people with severe and enduring mental health problems, access to which is made by an application system, after referral.

The Mill is a three story building on the Cowley Road, East Oxford, providing daytime social care and respite for local people suffering with severe and enduring mental illness. As well as providing a social network for service users there is a strong focus on creative pursuits – provisions are made for a range of activities in music and art. The Mill provides a flexible environment for people to express themselves creatively, encouraging them to use the equipment and art materials on offer.

At the back of the building, on the ground floor, past the communal kitchen and dining facilities, there is an impressive double-height studio space, with a pitched glass roof, that acts as a 'common room' and an art studio. 'Service users' – those who use the Mill – are free to exploit the space however they wish, although some prefer a more structured environment and, for those individuals, there are occasional classes, run by volunteers.

An 'art worker' oversees specific projects and offers advice to individuals on the practical elements of technique and production. There is no formal learning programme here but the classes that run in conjunction with a local gallery provide an education on the theory and history of art whilst helping those who attend to identify the cultural resources on offer in the local community. The overall intention is to broaden the perspective of individuals whose lives are relatively insular due to the emotional and physical restrictions of their illness.

Art materials for the Mill are bought with charity funds, with an emphasis on paint and canvas. The charity is now making a more determined effort to appeal to the community for direct donations that may bring about a diversity of media.

The Mill organisation relates to the charity-shopping public because it has set up a unique commercial gallery initiative for its users to exhibit and sell their artwork. The gallery opened in May 2008 with a launch exhibition, open to the public and promoted through mental health networks and other local groups. Two curated exhibition events have so far been hosted and a third is about to be installed, with a view to maintaining a programme of quarterly events.

The building itself has a large front window facing the street that is encased by white boards to create a 'white cube' in which to display artwork. The gallery space upstairs is shared between two rooms, and is used also for meetings and focus groups. The main room is painted white, benefits from natural light from a sash window at the front of the building and has been tailored for exhibitions with lighting that can be trained on individual artworks. A second room, painted a pale green colour, provides a supplementary show space. Large, lockable cupboards in both rooms supply valuable storage areas for canvases and furniture that is extraneous to art events.

The current group of artists who produce pieces for exhibition at The Mill work in a variety of media, but it was decided that the most recent exhibition would be limited to painting, whilst aiming to reflect the diversity within the discipline. With the exception of a couple of weeks' installation time, the works are left in situ between openings so that there is always artwork on display for the public to view and to purchase. The main gallery is currently exhibiting canvases. The second room has several framed paintings and one drawing. Predominant themes are birds and flowers but there are also several abstract works, all in a variety of sizes. Prices range from a modest £30 to £300, for the biggest and most detailed works.

Several artworks have been sold at The Mill's openings and afterwards. The staff encourage the artists to deal directly with interested patrons but they are also happy to mediate transactions, if necessary. The financial arrangement between artist and gallery is negotiated on an individual basis, fixed only to cover the charity's initial outlay costs of materials, upon sale of a work. Any contribution after that is a decision made at the artist's discretion.

In the future, The Mill plans to open its gallery resources to local artists and other community groups to raise additional income but, more importantly, to raise the profile of the initiative. The mental health service has, in the past, found itself ghettoised and it is vital to find ways of integrating itself into local community. Raising awareness of mental health issues and expelling myths through communication and understanding, is at the centre of the charity's ambition for this venture. It offers a positive face to the public whilst providing practical, social skills for the users. By visiting the exhibitions and purchasing the artwork, the public fulfills these aims.

ADDRESS The Mill, Oxfordshire Mind, 46 Cowley Road, Oxford OX4 1HZ
TELEPHONE 01865 721 458 OPEN to the public for viewing Monday to Thursday 10am - 3pm

Bryn Pistyll - Caernarfon, Wales

Antur Waunfawr is a leading social enterprise providing employment and training opportunities for people with learning disabilities in their own community.

Antur Waunfawr operates over four sites in and around Caernarfon. Bryn Pistyll is the original site of the community and is now its headquarters, located in Waunfawr. It provides social and therapeutic activities with a horticulture site, based in one of the most beautiful parts of the Gwyrfai valley, just outside Snowdonia National Park. The site is a popular attraction for local people and tourists, and includes a nature park, gardens and nursery, museum, crafts and local products shop, café and children's play area.

The establishment of Antur Waunfawr in 1984 stemmed from the vision of one man, R. Gwynn Davies, and the strong support he received from the people of the Waunfawr area. Twenty years ago he founded this charitable company, offering meaningful work to people with learning disabilities, as an alternative to institutionalised care within specialist centres. Antur Waunfawr demonstrated that, by providing opportunities for learning to disabled adults, they could live and work within their own communities and be accepted as equal citizens.

During the early years, people came to the village of Waunfawr to see this new philosophy at work, inspiring similar ventures. Now that the once pioneering concept has been widely accepted, visitors continue to come to Waunfawr and Caernarfon, not so much to study the operation, but rather because of the variety of services that are offered here. Over the years the business side of the organisation has developed and now more than seventy people are employed. As well as playing an important role in the wider community, Antur Waunfawr is also a key player in the regeneration of the local economy.

Within the surroundings of Bryn Pistyll there is a nature park and attractive gardens, transformed by the workers of Antur from seven acres of boggy ground. The park attracts all kinds of wildlife, and has secret paths, woodland and unusual works of art, set against spectacular mountain views. 'Ty Capel' (the old chapel house) hosts an exhibition to celebrate the life of local cartographer and explorer John Evans, the first man to map accurately the upper regions of the Missouri River. The gardens have an interesting and colourful array of flowers and the on-site nursery sells a good selection of home produced plants and flowers. The Blas y Waun Café offers tea and home-cooked meals.

The Bryn Pistyll Gift Shop sells a variety of crafts and local produce. A range of quality, handmade recycled paper and greeting cards are made by the crafts team. The group is currently working with the Park division to develop its own distinctive range of pottery for sale in the shop. A selection of jams and chutneys are produced on site and are also available in other commercial outlets in the local town of Caernarfon, with cafés and shops reporting a fast growing trade in the jams. The handmade cards and recycled paper are available by mail order.

The Bryn Pistyll craft shop is currently undergoing transformation into an historic village shop. A shop has operated on these premises, off the A4085 Beddgelert Road, since 1830. Run by the same family for over one hundred and fifty years, this link persists right through to the present day. Gwynn Davies, a descendant of the family, worked in the shop as a young boy. It stocked everything that a small-holder or quarryman might need around the beginning of the 20th century, from groceries such as tea and coffee, to clothing, boots and animal food. From the old shop and ruined cottages adjacent to it, Gwynn Davies turned his vision of a community enterprise into reality and Antur Waunfawr was formed. In 1992 it opened its doors again to the public, as a craft shop to this new venture.

Mr. Gwynn Davies died last year and Antur Waunfawr inherited many items from the original shop, some of it over one hundred and fifty years old. It was thought to be a fitting tribute to him to refit the shop to look as it would have done historically and to relay to the public an important part of the village history. Gwynn Davies' son, Gwion, still works at Antur and is able to remember his grandmother and great uncle running the shop. Together with the memories of local people, in particular the older members of the community, Antur is able to piece together an accurate impression of the sights, smells and sounds of the interior. Cutting down on packaging will liberate a mixture of aromas, including fresh coffee, fruit, paraffin and rubber as well as synchronising the shop with a modern concern for the environment.

The visitors' experience will begin with the sound of an old bell attached behind the front door, as customers enter through the portal that will transport them back in time to the original village shop. The first encounter will be of a small parlour or study room where the shopkeeper, a prominent man in the local community who served on various committees, would do the accounts. In the main shop, on the left side, the original wooden shelving will be stocked with period foods and articles. The shop will continue to stock its own produce, such as homemade jams and chutneys, traditional sweets and toffee, woodwork, traditional hardware goods, such as enamelware, and slatework, using local slate, all made by Antur workers. Also available will be books of local interest as well as Antur's own literature.

Antur Waunfawr does much to recycle, reuse and restore across all of its four sites. Warws Werdd is the Antur furniture shop on the Cibyn industrial estate, four miles away in Caernarfon (see 'Furniture'), and the Caergylchu project runs a Materials Recycling Facility with Cyngor Gwynedd, the local authority at Caernarfon.

ADDRESS Bryn Pistyll, Waunfawr, Caernarfon, Gwynedd LL55 4BJ TELEPHONE 01286 650 721 OPEN Monday to Friday 9am - 4pm

Paintings packaged in bubble wrap awaiting collection at Bethany Christian Trust, Edinburgh. ADDRESS 3 Morningside Road, Edinburgh EH10 4AY TELEPHONE 0131 477 2618 OPEN Monday to Saturday 9:30am - 5pm

Mind at The Mill, Oxford (see page 251)